D0407047

NEW
THOUGHT
for a NEW
MILLENNIUM

A

For Nicole—
Happy reading
Michael A. Mosley

NEW THOUGHT
for a NEW
MILLENNIUM

XII

Twelve Powers
for the
21st Century

XXI

Edited with an Introduction by
Michael A. Maday

UNITY VILLAGE, MISSOURI

First Edition 1998

Copyright © 1998 by Unity School of Christianity. All rights reserved. No part of this book may be used or reproduced in any manner whatsoever without written permission from Unity School of Christianity except in the case of brief quotations embodied in critical articles and reviews or in the newsletters and lesson plans of licensed Unity teachers and ministers. For information, address Unity Books, Publishers, Unity School of Christianity, 1901 NW Blue Parkway, Unity Village, MO 64056-0001.

To receive a catalog of all our Unity publications (books, cassettes, and magazines) or to place an order, call our Customer Service Department: (816) 969-2069 or 1-800-669-0282.

The publisher wishes to acknowledge the editorial work of Michael Maday, Brenda Markle, Raymond Teague, Sandy Price, and Stacey Rohr; the copyediting of Thomas Lewin; the production help of Rozanne Devine; and the marketing efforts of Allen Liles, Terri Springer, Karen King, and Sharon Sartin.

Cover illustration and design by
Gretchen West

The New Revised Standard Version was used for all Bible verses, unless otherwise stated.

Library of Congress Cataloging-in-Publication Data

New Thought for a new millennium : twelve powers for the 21st
    century / edited by Michael A. Maday.
        p.   cm.
    Includes bibliographical references (p.).
    ISBN 0-87159-205-3
    1. New Thought. 2. Unity School of Christianity—Doctrines.
    3. Christian life—Unity School of Christianity authors. I. Maday,
    Michael A.
    BX9890.U505N48 1998
    289.9'7—DC21   97-26296
                                           CIP

Unity Books feels a sacred trust to be a healing presence in the world. By printing with biodegradable soybean ink on recycled paper, we believe we are doing our part to be wise stewards of our Earth's resources.

*"It is the prerogative of Spirit
to know the future."*

—Charles Fillmore[1]

Table of Contents

FOREWORD   **1**
by Marianne Williamson

INTRODUCTION   **3**
TWELVE PATHWAYS TO A NEW MILLENNIUM   **4**
by Michael A. Maday

I. The Power of Love   **19**
IF LOVE LED THE WAY   **21**
by Jim Rosemergy

II. The Power of Faith   **37**
THE FIRE OF FAITH   **38**
by Rosemary Ellen Guiley

III. The Power of Understanding   **53**
UNDERSTANDING: ACCELERATION IN
SPIRITUAL INFORMATION   **54**
by Sir John Marks Templeton

IV. The Power of Wisdom   **71**
THE AGE OF WISDOM   **72**
by Eric Butterworth

V. The Power of Imagination   **85**
IMAGINATION: THE WONDROUS POWER
OF CONCEPTION   **86**
by James Dillet Freeman

VI. The Power of Zeal   **103**
ZEAL: A FUEL FOR SPIRITUAL PIONEERING   **104**
by Christopher H. Jackson

VII. The Power of Strength   121
     FINDING STRENGTH IN OUR BROKENNESS   123
          by Bernie Siegel, M.D.

VIII. The Power of Will   137
      WILL: THE FOUNDATION FACULTY
      OF THE NEW GLOBAL ORDER   139
          by Barbara King

 IX. The Power of Life   155
     TOWARD LIVING THE ABUNDANT LIFE   157
          by Joan Gattuso

  X. The Power of Power   173
     POWER SHIFT: A NEW PARADIGM
     FOR THE NEW MILLENNIUM   174
          by Robert Brumet

 XI. The Power of Renunciation   189
     A NEW HEAVEN AND NEW EARTH   190
          by Rosemary Fillmore Rhea

XII. The Power of Order   207
     DISCOVERY OF A NEW ORDERING OF THE FUTURE   209
          by Barbara Marx Hubbard

AFTERWORD   229

FURTHER READING   231

NOTES   233

FOREWORD

As we approach the end of the twentieth century, a huge and inexorable wave of consciousness is penetrating the Western mind. Our desires to create the most dynamic scenarios for twenty-first-century living move us headlong into the realization that the most forward-looking ideas are not necessarily new at all, but eternal principles which stand outside the circumstances of particular historical epochs. At this time of profound change from one millennium to another, we realize an extremely significant point: Some things never change.

Modern science itself now bolsters the tenets of faith, as we see expressed in quantum physics, as well as ancient religious philosophy, that the mind is indeed a supremely creative tool. Those of us who perceive the world metaphysically view human consciousness as a divine vessel. God has given us the freedom to think what we choose and the creative capacity to bring forth worlds accordingly. What we think, we shall experience, and when we think with God, we employ our capacity to cocreate a heaven on earth.

The powers of God are given to us to share with Him and all of creation, and our task is to learn those powers and express them diligently in our lives. This book is an aid to doing that.

Unity's *New Thought for a New Millennium* introduces and illustrates the twelve powers of humanity as expressed by Charles Fillmore, the co-founder of Unity School of Christianity. It invites us to go deeper to uncover the powers within ourselves. These are powers of consciousness, greater than the powers of technology, science, business, government, economics, or any other worldly expression. What this book shows us is that whatever power these worldly activities seem to possess, they derive from the powers of consciousness. What we are learning anew at this critical moment in world history is that, compared to the power of God, the power of the world is no power at all.

New Thought for a New Millennium is the gate to a future in which the face of God is clearer to the world. *It* has much to teach and *we* have much to learn. I believe that New Thought Christianity will be a hugely significant force in the twenty-first century. It presents an expression of the Jesus Christ teachings uncorrupted by the angry and judgmental projections of the last two thousand years. The veils are being lifted, and Unity is a lifter.

—Marianne Williamson
February 1997

Marianne Williamson is a philosopher, speaker, teacher, and author who, since 1983, has been speaking to packed houses in this country and abroad. She has done extensive charitable work for people with life-challenging illnesses.

Marianne is most acclaimed as an author. Her three books—*A Return to Love, A Woman's Worth,* and *Illuminata*—have all topped the *New York Times* best-seller list; *A Return to Love* was No. 1 for thirty-five weeks in 1992! She is also the author of a children's book, *Emma & Mommy Talk to God.* Her new book is *The Healing of America.*

INTRODUCTION

"The future is beyond knowing, but the present is beyond belief. We make so much noise with technology that we cannot discover that the stargate is in our foreheads. But the time has come; the revelation has already occurred, and the guardian seers have seen the lightning strike the darkness we call reality. And now we sleep in the brief interval between the lightning and the thunder."

—**William Irwin Thompson**[1]

Twelve Pathways to a New Millennium

Michael A. Maday

I t has been building these last few decades, a kind of millennial momentum that is easy to sense but difficult to comprehend. Just the approach of the year 2000 alone is probably enough to trigger millennial thoughts. We know from history that the approach of another thousand-year cycle has spawned numerous millennial movements. During the two centuries before the birth of Jesus Christ, the Jews experienced apocalyptic visions. Prior to the year 1000 C.E., the Joachimites and Free Spirits formed movements in medieval Europe, warning of destruction and transfiguration. So this time around, the arrival of a new millennium is bound to upset our sensibilities. For some reason innate to our incarnation, it is so easy for many to fear this event as some kind of ending. Who hasn't heard the prophecies of Nostradamus, Edgar Cayce, and others predicting massive Earth changes, political upheavals, wars, and devastation? You can hardly buy your groceries these days without some tabloid shouting out some horrific prediction. Recently I read we would know "the worst winter in 500 years!" Even our more credentialed media are filled with news that gives even the most sophisticated amongst us reason to pause. Unlike in the not so distant past, we have the intricate technologies of television and Internet to bring the pathos and tragedy of six billion human beings around the globe directly to our screens, placing them squarely and literally in our faces. Whatever we have gained in swifter and more comprehensive communication, we may have lost in the indiscriminate bulk of information, challenging us to keep it all in perspective, if we can.

But it seems quite a leap of illogic, as Mr. Spock might put it, to go from this year's hard winter or extraordinarily hot summer or the increase in hurricane intensity this past season—or the terrible news of some incident of racial violence and oppression—to thinking that this is all evidence of the end of the world.

Yet somehow the coming of a new millennium makes it easier to think it so. From the early Puritans' "errand into the wilderness" to the latest survivalist enclaved somewhere in Idaho, the notion of "endism" is rampant in America. The belief that we will somehow be purged in the fire of God's anger, that Jesus is returning, or that there's a new heaven and a new earth around the corner is prevalent. Suicide bombers say the end is near. Interest in neopagan rituals and alien abductions increases, all with an endist edge.

FUTURE IS AS FUTURE DOES

I remember having lunch with James Dillet Freeman, Unity's poet laureate, the man who has the distinct honor of having two of his poems taken to the moon, one each by two different astronauts. Since Jim is one of the authors in this anthology, I was encouraging him to speculate more about the future in his essay. He looked straight at me and said: "Mike, no one knows the future. We hardly know the present!"

Jim Freeman is right. The great seers and prophets of old and our more modern psychics and pundits notwithstanding, when we try to tell what the future will hold, we rarely can do more than provide an imaginative perspective on our present.

As an old science fiction fan, I'm used to speculating about the future. I began reading and raving about SF back when it wasn't as cool as it is today. I read the Robert A. Heinlein juveniles, the Allen E. Nourse and Paul French novels for adolescents while still a child. I read Heinlein's classic *Stranger in a Strange Land* in 1962, shortly after it first came out. I was at the tender age of thirteen, and it majorly influenced my life. I was a big fan of Isaac Asimov and Arthur C. Clarke as well as of Heinlein. I've been a Trekker since 1966, and when *2001: A Space Odyssey* first premiered in 1968, for me it was a religious experience.

So I've been focused on the future most of my life. This, as many used to remind me, is one way to escape the unpleasant details of one's present, and I do not deny that that was an important motivation. But to leave it at that, which is like dismissing science fiction as escapist fantasy, is to miss the values of learning to speculate, of deliberately keeping an open mind, of learning the art of intentionally suspending your disbelief. Speculating about the future can be an effective way of breaking the bondage of our past and opening ourselves to the realities of the present. My nearly fanatical interest in SF began to wane in the 1970s as I discovered spirituality. Learning to meditate and to experience new levels of expanded consciousness gave me a whole new understanding of what life can hold for us. What I used to grope for by reading and dreaming about the future, I began to receive in abundance by focusing clearly on the present, by learning to be here right now. I still like science fiction but I prefer to travel to the world inside of me, to know the upliftment and freedom that changing my consciousness gives me. Besides, as I grow older, the world resembles some aspects of the "future" of my youth; in other ways, of course, as one of my T-shirts says, "The future is not what it used to be!" (As I was writing this, I heard on National Public Radio that it was the "Awake Day" for the HAL 9000 computer in *2001*!) This, of course, is hardly surprising, since all speculations about the future are really investigations into our present. But whether our probes are deep enough to stand the test of time or whether they have a more ephemeral nature, it is important to remember what Jim Freeman was reminding me of, that we are speaking most emphatically about today.

Still, around us millennialism abounds. We can avail ourselves of the books, cassettes, and newspapers as well as the Web chat rooms that predict the end of the world, the massive Earth changes, the political and social chaos to come, the triumph of the righteous, and the loss of just about everyone and everything else. Is this stuff about the future—or does it have more to do with the past?

The very issues that make the headlines today, racial cleansings, abortion clinic bombings, homophobic demonstrations, and so on—the very "hot" issues that seem to fire the beliefs of all millennialists—may very well be symptoms of a different kind of ending: the end of archaic patterns of prejudice, limited thinking, and ignorance. The fire of these endings, which are now at their sunsets, may be enjoying one last glory before taking its place in the history of humanity's childhood.

Of course, unless you happen to be a true believer in some current millennial movement, it is also easy to ignore all this as just more quasi-religious nonsense. After all, we can reason, what's in a date, anyway? What makes a year a certain number? Isn't it all rather arbitrary and artificial? Our Gregorian calendar starts things off with the birth of Jesus. The Jews, the Muslims, and the Chinese have a different basis to do this accounting; for them it will just be another year. So when the Millennium hits, will it only impact us Gregorians? Will the others be spared the (future) shock waves?

Then we must acknowledge the unpopular fact that the new millennium does not begin January 1, 2000, but exactly one year later—January 1, 2001. The year 2000 is not the beginning of the third millennium, but the final year of the second. From this point of view, and it is legitimate, the coming of the new millennium is just one more orbit around the sun, just another year.

However, there is more to this millennium business than just what the date on the calendar is or what some ancient seers might have meant that could be relevant today. For one thing, it feels important, like when my car's odometer rolls over to show all zeros and I feel that vague sense of accomplishment! Furthermore, the turning of a century, let alone a millennium, seems to me to be a significant event for more pragmatic reasons, just like the coming of New Year's Day means more than the need to purchase a new calendar. Or when you turn thirty or forty or sixty-five, it is more than just another birthday, but, rather, the opportunity to take inventory of your life and make plans for the future. The coming of a new millennium brings our culture an opportunity to take stock, create a new vision for ourselves, and start over.

THE DAWNING OF AN AGE

"To discover the truth in anything that is alien, first dispense with the indispensable in your own vision."

—*Leonard Cohen*[2]

In 1972 I read a book entitled *The Transformation: A Guide to the Inevitable Changes in Humankind* by George B. Leonard. Like Heinlein's book I had read ten years earlier, this book changed my life. It helped draw me to Northern California, where I lived for seven years, drinking in the culture of the San Francisco Bay Area as if I were the proverbial sponge. There I learned a great deal about how to "dispense with the indispensable," including a healthy respect for how tough an assignment it really is. It helped me understand the late sixties, the counterculture, the rebellion of the times; I understand it now as part of a kind of millennial fever, part of the inevitable change in humankind. I began to see that, to a certain extent, California was a barometer for the nation as a whole and that the United States was the same for the rest of the world.

XII — 8 — XXI

The country was still gripped in the fervor of a kind of conversion. It was the "dawning of the Age of Aquarius." But then, as we all know, the idealism of the time had to deal with one crushing blow after another: Kennedy and King had been killed, Altamont had followed Woodstock, the Vietnam War escalated, the imminent Revolution seemed to be stalling out and slipping away. The '70s evolved into the time to discover yourself; the human potential movement and spirituality blossomed—but the sense of community languored. The '80s rekindled a new sense of an old energy, the desire to know earthly security and pleasures, to make it big and rich. With this new materialism replacing much of the old idealism for many, it became very fashionable to dismiss the ideals of universal freedom and love, to "trash the '60s." I called it the "dunning of the Age of Aquarius," but nobody laughed.

From the publication in 1980 of another watershed book, *The Aquarian Conspiracy* by Marilyn Ferguson, the '80s, somewhat paradoxically, also gave birth to the urge to network and to develop communities that built trust, shared information, and grew together spiritually. The counterculture became the "New Age."

This movement seemed to thrive despite or because of the massive cultural movement toward materialism. This clash was evident as the New Age hit the popular consciousness, and while channeling and psychics became more mainstream, a cynical backlash also developed.

The '90s seem to have been like a marriage of the last two decades, the challenge of making it work despite all the contradictions and gulfs of understanding. The New Age, maligned in name but powerful in spirit, has grown to include a national and global mix of diverse and creative cultural elements, all seeking a new way to make it work. Now, in the late-'90s, our marriage of practicality and idealism is about to be tested, for we are what President Clinton calls "a bridge to the twenty-first century." The millennium is at hand—and it may be our species' test of congruency between what we claim to believe and how we truly behave.

Interestingly, on January 23, 1997, the outer planets—Jupiter, Uranus, and Neptune—aligned themselves in a pattern so rare that it hadn't been seen in almost two hundred years. In fact, it had not been since the Renaissance that our five outermost planets aligned themselves in such harmony that, astrologically, the chart for the day showed a perfect six-pointed star. Many speculated that this could be the true dawning of the Age of Aquarius.

Whether you think astrology is bunk or a useful map of consciousness, whether you believe in it or not, what I think is significant is not the day January 23 itself, but what we all choose to do with the possibility it represents. Many people, including me, chose to join with the global community, which called the phenomenon "GaiaMind" and made this day a day of prayer and peace. "Gaia" is the Earth's very Spirit of life, and I think that any day which brings the world an excuse to pray together is a great day.

My point here is, whether the new millennium has any symbolic, mythic, or archetypal meaning on its own—or whether it's all in our own heads—it is an opportunity to start anew, to honor our pasts but to move on, to create a new age.

XII

10

XXI

> We're walking into a new century;
> We've been traveling now for millions of years.
> We've learned a great deal about how not to act;
> We've been responsible for so many tears.
> We don't have to learn that way anymore;
> We can leave our foolish ways behind.
> Like a prodigal child, we're waking up to ourselves,
> And I think we're liking what we find.
> We miss so many beautiful things,
> Preoccupied with building walls.

But now we know how freeing it is,
Every time another section falls.

—Doug Bottorff[3]

As Doug Bottorff sings in his album *One World*, we have the chance to do things differently now. We can look forward to this new period of history and make it something grand. Like the Star Trek universe, the future can be positive, humanity can learn to live in peace, negotiate consensus, and govern itself with community, respect for diversity, and peace. The human race is just now emerging from its childhood and its adolescence has barely begun, and it, while no doubt challenging and awkward at times, can also be an unprecedented opportunity for learning and maturation.

I personally believe that in years distant from now, it will be the twentieth century which will mark the beginnings of modern time. Perhaps future historians will target 1945, with its unleashing of atomic power; or 1957, with the launching of Sputnik. Maybe they will like a nice, round 1950—or maybe they'll like 2000, "twenty oh oh." The kids (in all of us) will have fun with that.

XII

11

XXI

THE NEW MILLENNIUM: THE BOOK

This book began as a vision on the part of the Operations Committee at Unity School of Christianity to present a more positive image of the future than members expected to see coming from our more conservative brethren. They wanted a statement from Unity and the New Thought movement that was a kind of antidote for all the apocalyptic nay-saying, a vision for the future that was optimistic and filled with the awareness that the presence of God is in all things. God was not bringing down the "end times" as punishment for our wickedness. Satan was not coming out of his thousand-year pit, to get his due—that's a misreading of the book of Revelation. God did not have a favored few who would be saved from some coming catastrophe, but was moving within each of us, bringing each of us to our "salvation," to our realization, however long that may take us, of our eternal oneness with the Divine.

To put it another way, we wanted a millennium book that told people that the power to affect their lives came from within them and not from some power from without. That is the message for the new millennium and the theme of this book.

I began meeting with Jim Rosemergy, executive vice president of Unity School; Bill Dale, senior director of Publishing; and Nancy Clark, who was then the senior director of Outreach; to brainstorm the concepts, possible authors, and potential market for this millennium book. We wanted the book to have a universal appeal, so we deliberately searched for a balance of authors from both inside and outside the movement. The result is that of the twelve authors of this book, seven are Unity ministers, but five are from outside of Unity—and it was with great joy that we welcomed a sixth, Marianne Williamson, who asked us if she might write the Foreword for the book.

For those new to both movements, both Unity and New Thought are outgrowths of the "mind cure" religious movement in the nineteenth century. Based in large part on the healing ideas of Phineas Quimby, but including, in generous measure, the Transcendentalism of Ralph Waldo Emerson as well as an emerging acquaintance with the philosophy and practices of yoga, New Thought includes within its umbrella Unity, Religious Science, Divine Science, Science of Mind, and other movements. Christian Science is distinctly separate, yet still a sister. In many ways, the New Thought movement is the forerunner of the current explosion of interest in spirituality and the New Age. The title of this book, *New Thought for a New Millennium*, is, in part, a playful reference to this movement; however, we do not mean to imply that this book speaks for the New Thought movement.

The Twelve Powers of Man

From the most ancient of times, when individual men and women cowered down and hid at the ferocious sounds that came in the night, human beings have wanted to name powers in their natural world. Some, they called *tiger;* others, *bear;* some, the *fertile soil;* others, the *nurturing sun;* and *the cool, mothering moon.* Magic and superstition combined with the infinite mystery of life and death to create myths and legends that themselves grew in power with the passing generations. Yes, we know about powers, we human beings; we have believed in them for thousands upon thousands of years!

Then there also have been our most ancient of adepts, wise beyond belief, who lived simply in the mountains of Tibet, the caves of India, or the savannahs of Africa and who turned within and saw for themselves their own divinity. They interpreted the subtle meanings they saw there and gave them to the rest of us to try to comprehend. They spoke of powers too, but these were the inner powers of surrender to our divinity and trust in the Source. We may not have understood the masters of old, but we have known, even if dimly, that there are powers hidden inside us—like magic, but better than mere magic—powers greater than we can know with our limited experience.

When I, as editor, contemplated the long list of ideals and social issues we wanted this book to cover, I prayed for a way that this all could come together. The idea of an anthology based on Charles Fillmore's concept of the twelve powers of man, the twelve powers of awakening humanity, came almost immediately to mind. Why not organize the book around the twelve powers, assign social issues that seem to belong to each power, and then find the authors who could write responsibly on those subjects? The result is the book you have in your hands.

Metaphysical Interpretation: A Lens

Charles Fillmore, Unity's co-founder along with his wife Myrtle, was a visionary and a futurist, as well as many other things. He wrote, "The subconscious realm in man has twelve great centers of action, with twelve presiding egos or identities."[4] This book, I feel, flows with the original pioneering spirit of Charles and Myrtle Fillmore. It is fitting that Charles' twelve-power concept—itself a visionary and evolutionary idea—be the framework upon which the individual visions of our twelve authors hang.

One of Charles' major contributions to New Thought was his unique development of metaphysical Bible interpretation. This symbolic way of interpreting certainly existed prior to Charles Fillmore, yet he brought a particular flair and power to it. Charles' system has been further developed by his followers, notably, Herbert Hunt, Ed Rabel, and Paul C. Barrett. In essence, metaphysical interpretation is an approach that balances both left and right brains, both our logical and intuitive sides. On one hand, we study the words of a Bible passage and learn their literal and symbolic meanings; we also study the history and culture of the time to gather further insight. However, on the other hand, we then stop and meditate on the symbols and meanings and pray for guidance; we allow a space to open within us for a new meaning to unfold! When it does, we have a metaphysical interpretation, and usually it will include a practical lesson for us to use in our lives today.

This book uses this form of interpretation as a lens to view the twelve powers, their origins in the Bible as well as their practical applications that are shown in the essays. If you would like to learn more about this powerful lens, I suggest you consult Alden Studebaker's *Wisdom for a Lifetime.*[5]

To understand the twelve powers, you have to know that they are twelve expressions of the one Power, the Christ within each of us. The twelve powers are: love, faith, understanding, wisdom, imagination, zeal, strength, will, life, power, renunciation, and order. What is meant by "the Christ" is "the fully awakened human being," the same as the Buddha-Mind or the higher Self, the indwelling Lord, Shiva, the Atman, to use words from a number of traditions. It is the state of consciousness within us that is completely one with God. Jesus, the man from Galilee, born in Bethlehem, realized his true spiritual nature and became the Christ. He became our Wayshower, showing us the way for each of us to know our Christ nature and to fully realize it.

When Unity and New Thought speak of the Christ, we do not generally have Jesus exclusively in mind. We are usually speaking of the divine potential that we are here on Earth to realize. Charles Fillmore saw twelve pathways for realization of this one Truth; they are twelve paths that lead to the one mountain.

Fillmore also saw the twelve disciples of Jesus as symbolically representing each of these twelve pathways, these twelve powers of the Christ. He believed that each disciple manifested one aspect of the Christ more perfectly than any other and connected that power to that disciple. Peter became Faith; James became Wisdom and Discrimination; John, Love; Andrew, Strength; and so on.

Charles Fillmore believed that the calling of the disciples had real spiritual significance, especially the calling of the first four. In Matthew 4:1–22 (RSV), Jesus calls Peter, James, John, and Andrew. In this book we will see how the powers these disciples represent play crucial roles with the other powers. Jesus tells Simon Peter and his brother Andrew, "Follow me, and I will make you fishers of men." In Luke 5:4 (RSV), Jesus tells Simon Peter, "Put out into the deep and let down your nets for a catch." This can be interpreted to mean that as humanity develops out of mere personal awareness into spiritual consciousness, we must evolve deeper and larger powers. By following the lead of the Christ, we develop our spiritual powers.

In Matthew 19: 26–28 (RSV), Jesus says, "With God all things are possible." Peter responds by reminding Jesus that he and all the disciples have left everything and followed him. He asks Jesus what they will have. Jesus replies, "Truly, I say to you, in the new world, when the Son of man shall sit on his glorious throne, you who have followed me will also sit on twelve thrones, judging the twelve tribes of Israel." Those who fully know their Christ nature will fully master the twelve powers of life and consciousness.

Twelve is a symbolic number in the Bible and in much of the ancient world. In addition to the twelve disciples and twelve tribes of Israel, there are twelve sons of Jacob, twelve stones in the altar, twelve spies of Moses, twelve stars in the bride's crown, and twelve kinds of fruit on the tree of life. Of course, we know of the twelve months of the calendar and twelve signs of the zodiac, twelve inches to a foot, twelve units in a dozen, and so on. In addition, many ancient pantheons consisted of twelve gods and goddesses.

Twelve, as a symbol, means "completion." To me, this means we need not get hung up over whether there are really twelve powers or actually more or less—just as we know there must have been more than twelve historical disciples of Jesus. The point is that here is a map of twelve pathways to completion, the realization of our innate perfection, the actualization of our Christ nature. Let's not argue about the map; let's get to our destination. There we are likely to know the answer, not before.

Furthermore, just as Jesus tended to send his disciples out two by two (Luke 10:1) or in other combinations greater than one, the powers themselves do not truly work in isolation. If you contemplate it, you can see that the power of love needs the power of divine discrimination, of wisdom, to complement it. Faith works wonderfully well with understanding; imagination is activated by the power of order, and so on. In reality, all the powers are always at work, even when one seems to be predominating; all are really the Christ power manifesting itself in differing ways.

This overlapping of powers can be seen in the essays of this book. Each essay was written independently, yet you can see for yourself how the one Christ power keeps emerging time and again in different disguises. The Christ is the vine, the powers are the branches, and the branches tend to intertwine! As you are reading, remember to track these discussions as differing expressions of the One Power and One Presence, the Christ. I have introduced each essay with a brief description of its accompanying power, along with some metaphysical commentary that I hope will help you bring the book together as a whole.

At the back of the book, I've included a bibliography of books that have been written about the twelve powers. Some are still in print; many are not. But if you are intrigued by this ancient concept in modern guise, know that you can read beyond this book.

Having thus introduced the concept, I must also acknowledge that this book is not primarily a book on the twelve powers. It is a book about the new millennium as seen through the lens of the twelve powers of awakened humanity. However, it can serve as an introduction to the Fillmorean concept and as a kind of contemporary commentary on it.

Ostensibly, this book is about the future, but it is really about the present. As you read earlier, this is all we can hope for in speculative writing: to write deeply and meaningfully about the present. If we can uncover the seeds of the future that lie buried deep in the present, then we can tenderly nourish and encourage them to grow into a future we envision. In a very real sense, the future only lives in the present. As William Irwin Thompson's quote puts it at the beginning of this essay, we are living now in the brief interval between the lightning flash and the thunder. Let's not live in the deep slumber of ancient fears, but in open anticipation of the next phase of God's great emerging plan for humankind.

I hope this book inspires you to reflect deeply about humanity's present and recognize the seeds of our future that lie dormant within us. May they germinate and grow, one whole person at a time, a bright and prosperous future for all of our global family.

A FEW ACKNOWLEDGMENTS

I especially want to thank Allen Liles, the current senior director of Outreach, for his support. I also thank Gayle Revelle, my former associate editor, for our numerous discussions early in the development of this project. I thank Laura Barrett for loaning me her materials on the twelve powers and Melissa Bowers for her editorial assistance. I am indebted to Garth Matthes and my therapy training group, both in Kansas City and Eureka Springs, for their insights and support. I am also grateful to Carolyn Myss whose work on the powers within the body-mind could not have been better timed for me. Most of all, I want to thank Gurumayi for always being in my heart, guiding my powers to their fullest expression.

XII

18

XXI

Michael A. Maday is the editor of Unity Books and of this anthology. Michael was ordained in 1984 and served ministries in Pontiac and Flint, Michigan. He speaks regularly at the Unity Village Chapel at Unity Village, Missouri, as well as at centers around the country.

A former publisher of personal computer magazines and a secondary school teacher, Michael has a bachelor of arts degree in the social sciences from Oakland University in Rochester, Michigan. A student of yoga and meditation, he presently is receiving training in body-centered Gestalt psychotherapy. Published in *Unity Magazine,* Michael is preparing a book on practical Christianity for publication.

CHAPTER I

THE POWER OF LOVE

To the best of my knowledge, if there is one person who most deserves the credit for this book, it is Jim Rosemergy. So, although it is traditional to start out any discussion on the twelve powers with the power of faith, it is fitting that Jim's essay leads the way. It is traditional because Peter, who represents faith in Charles Fillmore's metaphysical system, was the first disciple chosen by Jesus. However, John, who represents the divine power of love, was known as the disciple whom Jesus loved, and if Jesus' gospel could be put into one word, that word would be *love*.

Divine love is a great healing and harmonizing force, for it sees good everywhere and in everyone.

"Imagine the world," Jim Rosemergy asks of us, "if love led the way." He calls love, after Robert Browning's poem, the "imprisoned splendor." Since Jim doesn't quote it in its entirety and since it is one of my favorite poems, I'll quote it here.

> Paracelsus
>
> Truth is within ourselves; it takes no rise
> From outward things, whate'er you may believe.
> There is an inmost center in us all,
> Where truth abides in fulness; and around,
> Wall upon wall, the gross flesh hems it in,

This perfect, clear perception—which is truth.
A baffling and perverting carnal mesh
Binds it, and makes all error; and to know
Rather consists in opening out a way
Whence the imprisoned splendor may escape,
Than in effecting entry for a light
Supposed to be without.[1]

I don't know of a better or more eloquent expression of the divine power within us. It clearly describes the kind of spiritual vision that this book is about and which we believe the next millennium will demonstrate.

If Love Led the Way

Jim Rosemergy

I wish I could look ahead a thousand years and see myself standing with my fellow human beings on the threshold of the thirty-first century. You might say, "Jim, wait a minute. What happened to the last thousand years? Let's not get too far ahead of ourselves. The twenty-first century hasn't even begun yet."

True, but if I knew what was ahead for us in the third millennium, I could tell you. I could look back at its history and see the decision points, crucial crossroads, and special insights that helped shape us and carry us forward. My thoughts on love's role in the next thousand years would be accurate. I would generate no false hope, for what I write of the future would have been confirmed by a look at the past, but because I am not standing on the threshold of the thirty-first century, I can only imagine.

Imagine the world if love led the way—a world without war . . . swords pounded into plowshares . . . families knowing nothing of famine. Life has been simplified, so family members can spend time together. The circle that is the family is joined, because the parents are no longer driven by "making ends meet." Prejudice is a past memory kept alive only so that it will not come again. The many races and cultures are blended together like wildflowers on a hill. Religions, if there are many, pray and worship with one another.

Humankind has experienced a spiritual awakening that began when we opened our hearts to one another.

I don't know what lies ahead for us, but I know my hopes. I also know our human tendencies for avarice and self-indulgence. The good news is that I am also aware of our spiritual tendencies. We can live lives that make it evident we were created of the dust of the earth, but we have the capacity to shake the dust from our feet and walk in love's way.

Some doomsdayers will tell us what lies ahead if we follow our human tendencies, but I want to see where our spiritual tendencies are taking us. If love charted the way for the next thousand years, what would happen? What new insights would dawn in us and be put to the test? What false premises would be put to rest? What would the challenges be? Would there be key moments for the human family, crossroads where critical choices are made?

Come, let us roam in a time that has not yet come. Let us look at our spiritual future, shake the dust from our feet, and follow love's lead. Although this path seems unknown to us, I believe it is written on our hearts.

XII
—
22
—
XXI

A False Premise

Our journey begins in 1953. During this year, Dr. John Bowlby, a British physician, published findings revealing the life-giving power of love. In orphanages, Bowlby observed infants and toddlers who failed to develop physically and mentally. Investigations determined that the children were being given the basic necessities of life. They were cleansed and fed, but were left unattended for extended periods of time. Because of the workload of the staff, there was little time for human contact and the play afforded children in a family. Bowlby concluded that the children failed to develop normally because they were not being picked up, cuddled, played with, and loved.

Practices changed at the orphanages. The children were given attention in addition to basic care, and they grew strong and began to develop their mental powers. It was an affirmation of the need for human contact, tenderness, and love.

This is a revealing story, but for an unknown reason, I doubted Dr. Bowlby's conclusion. I could understand the need for human contact, but something seemed amiss to me, and I did not know what it was.

The premise was that the children needed to be loved. This conclusion seemed obvious. Who could doubt it? It was a fact known for thousands of years. We crave human contact and yearn for love. However, when love leads the way, another premise is born.

A New Premise for the Twenty-First Century

Nearly every culture puts great credence on love. It is the thread woven through the many religions of the world. Jesus gave a simple commandment: "Love one another" (Jn. 15:17). The Jews follow love's way: "You shall love the Lord your God with all your heart, and with all your soul, and with all your might" (Deut. 6:5). Hindus likewise give allegiance to love: "Show love to all creatures and thou wilt be happy; for when thou lovest all things, thou lovest the Lord, for he is all in all" (Tulsi Das Hindu spirituality). It is also true of the Buddhists: "As a mother, even at the risk of her own life, protects her son, her only son, so let him cultivate love without measure toward all beings" (*The Sutta Nipata*).

Every human being wants to be cherished. Some of us hardly seem alive when we are alone and without someone to love us. Many of our songs echo this sentiment, for our voices have joined in a chorus that sings, "I can't live without you." How natural it was for Dr. Bowlby to conclude that the children were not developing normally because they needed to be loved. However, it was not true.

XII
—
23
—
XXI

A new insight of the third millennium is that our greatest need is not to be loved, but to love. The children in the orphanages were denied love, but more critical was the fact that they were denied the opportunity to express love. Their bodies may have been small, but they were spiritual beings made in the image and likeness of Love. Their nature was love. Their isolation did not allow them to be loving, and this is what stunted their growth.

The truth is we do not need to be loved to survive, grow, and thrive. We need to be loving. Love is within us. We are not empty of it when we are born. We are little bundles of love. Life is a joy and wonder when we allow love to escape from within us. Love's expression calls forth our growth and development. It paves the way for us to become what God has created us to be.

Love, the "Imprisoned Splendor"

As children, many of us had a favorite stuffed animal. We insisted for years that the "creature" was alive and that it loved us. Adults delight in children loving their inanimate friends, but the truth is that stuffed animals contain no love. It seems blasphemous to even write such words, but we all know it is true. The stuffed animals I played with as a child are probably saying, "Tell us it isn't true!" However, isn't it interesting that we felt love when we hugged our stuffed animals? This was particularly true when we had been feeling emotional pain.

Where does the love come from? Is it from our inanimate friends? No, the love we feel comes from within us. The "imprisoned splendor" of which the poet Robert Browning wrote in his poem "Paracelsus" is released from its prison in the soul. We loved our friend when we were children, and we felt alive.

The happiest, most respected people on earth are those who know love is the answer, but they have ceased looking for it. They have found love within themselves. Perhaps it came in moments of silent reflection, but life has taught them that love is experienced when it is released and shared with the world.

Celebrities are often showered with love and adoration from others. Some of the people are close friends, and others are the nameless public. It is difficult to understand when one of these talented and cherished people commits suicide. Obviously, being loved is not enough.

Being truly alive means being loving. This is the message of the children in the orphanages. They were saying to us, "Love us if you will, but please give us an opportunity to love you." This is a message we hear when love leads the way.

Often when I speak to audiences about these things, I see smiles and heads nodding in agreement. Then I say, "And yet, if I asked you to turn to your neighbor and hold her face gently in your hands and say to that person, 'I love you. I really love you,' many of you would feel uncomfortable. In fact, I'll bet many of you are experiencing an increased heart rate because you are concerned that I may ask you to do such a thing." Usually, nervous laughter moves through the audience. Our reluctance to let love out does not deny that love is our nature. It alarms us that love is an "imprisoned splendor."

The Challenge of Every Age

No one who is filled with anger, resentment, or hate develops naturally. These strong human emotions disrupt the harmonious functioning of the body and make loving relationships with other people nearly impossible, but their greatest impact is that they stand guard and keep the splendor of love imprisoned. This is the challenge of every age—forgiveness.

It is easy to love those who love us. These people are being true to their nature, and through their words and actions, they call us to a life of love. The challenge is to love those who dislike us, have harmed us, or have harmed our loved ones.

XII

25

XXI

Forgiveness is the challenge of every age, and it is a call to return to love. It is love in our souls saying, "Release me; let me go. My home is in your soul, but my work is in the world."

I have a friend whose wife was murdered. I cannot imagine the pain and anguish he must have felt, and yet my friend refused to personally press charges against the murderer and went and forgave the one who had killed his wife. Even in the midst of indescribable pain, we are capable of love. It is an expression of Booker T. Washington's words, "Let no man pull you so low as to make you hate him."

A hurtful relationship is always a crossroads. It is a bitter road we take when we imprison love and hold on to anger and resentment. But when love leads the way, we find peace and much more, for each time we forgive, we awaken to our spiritual nature. We discover the best that we can be.

Forgiveness, the return to love, is needed in the twenty-first century. As I write, the age-old conflict between Arabs and Jews rages on. Some of their leaders are answering the challenge of every age—forgiveness—but others think that revenge is the answer and that annihilating the adversary will bring peace. When we believe this way, we remember our pain and suffering and forget that our nature is love.

Governments cannot forgive one another; their people can. Nations can embrace, but first, one person must return to love. This was done in 1904. Argentina and Chile had never been at war, but at the turn of the century they stood on the brink of a deadly conflict. The armies confronted one another, and war seemed imminent. In Buenos Aires, Monsignor Benavente captured the hearts of the people by preaching a sermon of peace. News of his appeal for peace reached Chile, and a bishop initiated a call for the end of tension. They continued their efforts until the people of the nations began to think peace instead of war. Eventually, the governments consented to arbitration by King Edward VII of Great Britain. A treaty was signed, but the commitment to peace did not end with the signing of the document.

The weapons poised on the borders were melted down, and a bronze statue of Jesus was cast. The right hand was extended as a blessing, and the left hand held a cross. This mammoth figure was carried on gun carriages and placed at the 13,000-foot level of the mountains that formed the border between the two countries. On March 13, 1904, it was dedicated. Standing before the figure, one can read these words: "These mountains themselves shall fall and crumble to dust before the people of Chile and the Argentine Republic forget their solemn covenant sworn at the feet of Christ."

What was done in 1904 will be done again. Statues may not be built, but individuals will step forward and say, "Enough of this pain. We will hurt one another no more."

GREATER LOVE THAN THIS

A young boy's older brother was ill and needed a blood transfusion. Tests showed that the boys had the same blood type, so the doctor explained the transfusion procedure to the younger boy and, with the parents' help, asked if he would give his blood for the transfusion. The boy seemed startled, but he agreed.

On the day of the transfusion, both boys lay on adjacent tables, and the transfusion began. After a short time, the young lad said to the physician, "When am I going to die?" The doctor explained that he was not going to die and that he would be fine, but then the physician realized the implication of the question. The boy thought that by giving his blood for the transfusion, he was giving his life for his brother. This is love's greatest expression. Of this Jesus said, "Greater love has no man than this, that a man lay down his life for his friends" (Jn. 15:13 RSV).

Love is willing to do extraordinary things. It forgets itself and the soul's anguish and affirms the value of other people and their pain. Most of us will never have the opportunity to give our lives for others, but all of us have the opportunity to give up our anger and resentment. I believe this is the way we were created to be. Loving with abandon is our spiritual tendency. Apparently, the expression of love is more important than our earthly life.

If the age of love is to dawn during the next thousand years, we are to put aside the false premise that we have to be loved to be fully alive. Love does not need to be added to us. Love is our nature, and it is destined to overflow as encouraging words, helping hands, and acts of kindness and compassion. We are not empty of love, but we do not experience it and become truly alive until love overflows from within us. This is a foundational ideal of the next millennium.

The First Law of Love

If we are willing to follow love's lead, a race of beings without prejudice will inhabit the earth at some time during the next millennium. They will be like a new species of humanity, compared to what we have commonly known. This new species of humanity will practice love's first law—acceptance.

Humanity mistakenly believes that love's first law is compassion. We want God to do something, usually to act on our behalf or on the behalf of a loved one. We may even ask why the Creator does not do something about wars and the world's suffering. We wonder if God really cares, if God loves us. We ask, "Wouldn't a God who is love itself do something about the anguish of the planet?"

I suspect Spirit's answer is not what we want to hear: "You started the wars; you end them. You have the means to alleviate the suffering; do it. Your barns are filled with grain while the children die of starvation. Open your hearts and release the love that is within you."

When love first escapes from its prison in us, its first action is acceptance. Condemnation ceases. We no longer demand change. We accept people the way they are. God loves us in the same way. The Presence does not demand that we change. If it is war we want, we can have it. God does not say, "I'll love you if you do it My way." We are accepted and loved just the way we are. Thank God, God's loving us does not depend upon our actions. Likewise, our loving others should not depend upon what other people do. It depends upon us.

A world without prejudice is our spiritual tendency and therefore our destiny. We are called to accept ourselves and others. In fact, I believe our many differences are part of the divine plan. They are our opportunity to look beyond appearances and to put into practice love's first law—acceptance.

All human beings share common ground, and it is more than planet Earth. Our language, skin color, religion, and culture may differ, but these differences provide us with an opportunity to practice acceptance and eventually honor what is valued by our fellow human beings. The common ground is no longer the dust that clings to our feet. It is the high regard and love we hold for one another.

We will learn about the different beliefs and cultures. Cultural exchange becomes the work of the many, rather than a government program that a few may share. It seems natural that eventually the cultures will be blended and something new will emerge. I do not believe we will adopt the practices of a particular culture, but as the millennium progresses, a new culture will come into being. Basically, a new species of human being will emerge. This one will look similar to us, but its values will be grounded in spiritual Truth. The being of the third millennium will find its oneness through its diversity.

The signs are with us now. Corporations are providing their associates with training that fosters an appreciation of our varied cultures and ethnic backgrounds. World travel and increased immigration are bringing us closer to one another. For a time, our differences may seem to intensify, but with love leading the way, we will learn to accept one another. Then we will discover our likenesses and our common spiritual roots.

Can you see the pattern emerging? Love is our nature, and it is to be released from within us. I believe a new species of human being is to be born in the next millennium. Our evolution over millions of years has brought us to this moment and filled it with promise. Unforgiveness and prejudice are two sentinels standing as barriers to love's emancipation and the emergence of the new species.

We are capable of giving our lives for others. Let us also be willing to give up our anger and resentment, so that unforgiveness no longer stands at the doors of our souls. This is work that each of us can do, and it contributes to the evolution of the race. As illustrated by my friend whose wife was murdered, our capacity to forgive is beyond imagining.

If we look closely at the second sentinel, prejudice, we will notice that this one who looks so stern is trembling with fear. He fears what is seemingly not like him. He has failed to accept himself, and therefore he cannot accept others. Appearances rule his world, so his world is limited to what he sees and thinks is right. Acceptance is his road to freedom, but his acceptance does not begin with those he has demeaned. It must begin with himself.

Marriage: Dead or Alive?

There are some who believe marriage is dead. They don't believe in it or find it necessary. They view marriage as something created by a legal document recorded at the courthouse, rather than something ordained by Spirit.

Strange, but when I think of marriage, I don't think of the legal document I signed over twenty-seven years ago. I have not looked at it since our wedding day. I don't even know the location of the courthouse where it is recorded; however, what has been recorded indelibly upon my soul is my love and adoration for my wife Nancy. You see, when I think of marriage, I think of love.

Many people have asked Nancy and me to tell them how to make a marriage work. We usually look at each other and shrug our shoulders and say that we don't know how. Maybe an unwillingness to intellectualize love is at the heart of a powerful relationship.

XII
30
XXI

Wiser people than I share helpful ideas about how to live in love. They probably say that it takes work, and they are correct, but I hope they don't imply working on the other person. Marriage demands that we work on ourselves. This is necessary for harmonious relationships in general, but the wonder of marriage is that we have a committed friend to help us. However, marriage is more than a lifelong self-improvement course, much more.

The new species of the next millennium will take little for granted. When love leads the way, we become explorers. In the coming century, we will return to the spiritual roots of marriage. In past centuries, humanity has explored prearranged marriages and, for the most part, found this practice wanting. In the twentieth century, we have explored multiple marriages and no marriage, or "living together." Now it is time to explore not marriage and its form, but its purpose and the purpose of loving relationships in general.

I don't believe marriages are "made in heaven." I believe they are *bound* for heaven. Loving another person is an important part of humankind's search for God. Nancy and I share a quest for the Infinite. Our commitment to this purpose enlivens us and brings us closer and closer together. This is the way it is when two people share a grand mission. Even the challenges of daily living can bring a greater realization of oneness. However, not all couples share this vision of a search for God, and it is not necessary that they do.

The reason is that at the heart of a loving relationship is the discovery of the Divine within the one with whom we share our life. Years ago, I wrote a poem to Nancy on Christmas day. It illustrates the discovery of the presence of God in our loved one. Since it was first written, I have changed the title to "To a Friend," for the truth embodied in the words is appropriate for any two people.

> There was a time when I thought
> God walked beside you,

But now I see God moves
with every step you take.
There was a time when I thought
God loved you,
But now I feel you are the love
I often speak of.
There was a time when I thought
God had blessed you,
But now I know
You are His blessing to me.

I believe that God indwells each person. Marriage and friendship ask us to search for and find God in our partner while our partner is searching for the same treasure in us. And just to make it interesting, we have in-laws and have to take out the trash, raise children, and find the balance of work, play, and family. All of these responsibilities can seem all-consuming, but in the next millennium, we will remember that when we commit ourselves to a life of love, we have committed ourselves to finding God in our partner.

I remember a time when I felt nearly overwhelmed by my love for Nancy. I pondered how I could feel such oneness with someone who had been a complete stranger. Then it dawned on me that this is one of the profound lessons of a spiritual joining. If we can feel at one with a person who was once a stranger, can we not experience oneness with the human family, for everyone we love was once a stranger? When we answer *yes*, love has led us deep into the mystery of marriage. Our love for our spiritual partner becomes a cup overflowing into the world. It is marriage that fills the cup, and God who causes it to overflow.

The Twenty-First-Century Family

Opportunities to learn love's way are everywhere, but nowhere more frequently than in the family. I suspect that many of the world's problems continue because we have not accepted the opportunity to learn the mysteries of love in the family setting. In fact, the limitations and false premises we hold about love are often passed from one generation to the next.

In the third millennium, I believe love will become a priority for the family. An early sign is with us now. Family members are spending more time together. Love seems more present and, certainly, more a force for good in our lives when we are present with one another.

Recently, I have seen in the media and witnessed first-hand, people who are simplifying their lives so they can spend more time together. These courageous forerunners of the new millennium are forsaking career paths that put work at the center of their lives. They have concluded that making ends meet is of little value if family relationships are tattered and torn. These people are putting family first. It is because they know they have great love to share with one another. They realize that the time with children is precious and limited.

Schools prepare the mind by teaching the facts and also by requiring that the student learn to think. Churches teach values and spiritual principles in a short encounter with the family each week. These institutions are foundational pillars of our society, but they are not the force for good that the family can be. Understanding values and the current "truths" are important, but we learn best from experience and by example. This is where the family can excel. I suspect that the world we imagine in our best moments depends upon the home becoming a place where love is "taught" every day.

This requires that family members simply spend time together. This commitment, combined with a willingness to let love lead the way, will transform individuals and be a forerunner to the discovery of not just the wonders of the family unit, but the human family.

XII

—

33

—

XXI

If Love Leads, Will Religions Follow?

It is natural to assume that religions will lead us into the next millennium. I hope they do, but if they continue to hold up their differences and declare that they know the only way, *we* must assume the reigns of leadership.

The challenge of religion is that it tends to become complicated. Its beliefs, creeds, and directives from world headquarters become a maze for the believer, rather than a clear path. The commentary on the scripture grows and the many words become a burden for people who are seeking the way of the heart. Perhaps these are odd words for a minister and author to write, but I believe I speak for many when I say that we are searching for a simpler way.

In my travels, I have met wonderful people. Supposedly, I went to teach them, but I left with greater understanding. I discovered that the people who are living profound lives are those who live a simple truth. One person values friendship above all. Everyone he meets is his friend. I call this person my best friend, and I am sure there are many who feel the same way. For another person, knowing the Truth is all-consuming, and for yet another, a life of prayer makes life meaningful. Others have decided to follow the Golden Rule or to adopt an attitude of service in all that they do. At the heart of their lives is a single ideal.

I am sure there are many guiding principles that are worthy of our attention, and by living them, we will find meaning and contribute to the world. Perhaps this is why there are many religions and so many approaches to God and successful living. Not all of us walk the same path, but all spiritual paths lead to the same place.

I am not sure whether love is a path or whether it is the place to which all paths lead, but I do know that many of the religions of the world proclaim love to be the answer.

A Crossroads

My life is now at a crossroads, for I have a choice to make. Writing these words over the course of several months has put love at the center of my life. It has dominated my thoughts and forced me to ask myself probing questions. It is as if each question were a road of the intersection and I were standing in the center. There are several paths to take.

As I look around, I see that I am not alone. You, the reader, are with me. Let us answer the questions together. Is love imprisoned in us, or is it emerging as a blessing to the human family? Are we looking for love, or are we willing to be loving? Are we accepting of others just the way they are? Have we accepted the challenge of every age and returned to love through forgiveness?

Every individual must answer these crossroads questions. Long ago one person must have let love lead the way, and love began to emerge. Most likely, forgiveness of self or another was required as a first step. Then this soul, free of anger and resentment, was able to accept others, rather than trying to change them. In this moment, a new species was born, the being whom Love had created. We are descendants of this one who decided to let love lead the way. We are children of Love.

A Little Child Shall Lead Them

President Lincoln's Emancipation Proclamation freed the slaves, but the quest for liberty continues. Freedom hardly ever comes in a day.

Love has proclaimed its emancipation from the chains of resentment and prejudice that live in humanity. Perhaps we can feel the tension or unrest of being called to a life of love. It demands that we let go of old ways of thinking and behaving, but let us remember that love is our nature and loving our destiny.

It is written, "The wolf shall dwell with the lamb . . . and a little child shall lead them" (Is. 11:6 RSV). This is a vision of the third millennium. Let us place our hands in the hand of the child and be led, for the name of this little one is "Love."

Jim Rosemergy was ordained a Unity minister in 1976. He has served ministries in Raleigh, North Carolina (a ministry that he pioneered); Spokane, Washington; and Kansas City, Missouri (at the founder's church, Unity Temple on the Plaza). A past president of the Association of Unity Churches, he currently serves as executive vice president of Unity School of Christianity at Unity Village, Missouri.

Jim is the author of numerous books: *A Recent Revelation, Living the Mystical Life Today, The Watcher, Transcendence Through Humility, A Daily Guide to Spiritual Living, A Closer Walk With God, Even Mystics Have Bills to Pay,* and *The Sacred Human.* His newest is *The Quest for Meaning: Living a Life of Purpose* for the Unity Movement Advisory Council's continuing *Quest* series.

CHAPTER II

THE POWER OF FAITH

"You gotta have faith!" So the saying goes. In fact, it is true that we do have faith—but faith in what? Faith in our fears, faith in our failures? We are always exercising our power of faith, but it is wise to contemplate in what direction we are moving.

If it weren't for faith, we could barely move. Our faith in gravity as well as in our own experience helps calm our fear that during our next step our feet might fly out from underneath us. Our faith in human training and learning helps us proceed through the intersection on a green light. Our faith in love helps us risk another relationship—or just open our hearts enough to feel the presence of another.

Our faith in God helps us be willing to bear all things. If love can lead the way, faith gives us the ability to love. Faith is the perceiving power of our minds, and it brings the power to shape our lives.

Faith is linked to the disciple Peter, the rock upon which Jesus built his church. Peter was originally called Simon, which means "hearing, or the receptive quality of the mind." Simon needed to be receptive to discern Truth and become Peter, the rock, the foundation of our spiritual lives. However, faith is more than just a passive rock; it can also be molten lava. It is a fire of transformation!

The Fire of Faith

Rosemary Ellen Guiley

In every age, our perception of the qualities of faith changes in accordance with the times. During the ministry of Jesus, faith was likened unto a rock—the rock upon which Jesus declared he would build his church. Over the course of time, we have envisioned faith similarly as a steadying influence: calm, solid, unwavering, deep, and still. All of these qualities continue to hold fast. But for the new era of the twenty-first century, faith is more energetic and active: it is a fire.

The fire of faith empowers and energizes. It purifies. It makes the torch that lights our daily lives and our spiritual path. It emblazons the way to God. The fire of faith calls us to action. The road ahead of us is clear. We must use faith to erase fear. We must use faith to heal. We must use faith to work miracles.

Faith operates in all aspects of life, not just spiritual. We need faith in order to manage our lives. We place our faith in certain laws of nature. We have faith in ourselves and in our abilities, talents, and skills. We have faith in our personal relationships. There is not one aspect of life that does not require faith in order to function at its optimum. When tragedy strikes, when the world turns upside down, it is faith that sees us through.

The best definition of faith can be found in the Bible, in Hebrews 11. The letter to the Hebrews was written to a group of early

Christians so discouraged that they were on the verge of giving up their new religion. The anonymous author of the letter exhorts them to hold on, for oftentimes we cannot see what we strive for, and we lose hope, when instead we should persevere. The goal, the reward, has not gone away, but is merely momentarily out of sight. If we stay to the path, it will reappear around the next bend. "Now faith is the assurance of things hoped for, the conviction of things not seen. . . . By faith we understand that the world was created by the word of God, so that what is seen was made out of things which do not appear" (Heb. 11:1, 3 RSV).

Similarly, Charles Fillmore defined faith as "the perceiving power of the mind linked with a power to shape substance. It is spiritual assurance, the power to do the seemingly impossible."[1]

Faith moves in the realm of the unseen. It cannot be measured, captured, rationed, or held. It moves us out of the plane of the material and into the plane of the universal Mind. As one gnostic gospel put it, "From the invisible he made all things visible, himself being invisible" (2 Enoch 18:5). Through faith, we come to terms with one of the fundamental metaphysical laws of the universe, that thought creates reality. What we think becomes manifest. What we believe comes to pass. How well and how quickly these manifestations occur depend upon our faith. With faith, we are empowered to make the invisible visible. We can pull our hopes and dreams from the intangible into the tangible.

Faith is the engine that drives our existence. Without faith, we are not motivated to believe anything, do anything, accomplish anything. "According to your faith be it done to you," said Jesus (Mt. 9:29 RSV). The greater our faith, the greater results we obtain, the greater works we do.

Faith has existed from the first moment of creation. "The look which goes from God into the soul is the beginning of faith whereby I believe things not revealed to me," said the Neoplatonic scholar Pseudo-Dionysius. Faith awaits our discovery. And once we discover faith, we must continually nourish it. If we do not nourish it and use it daily, it weakens, like an unused muscle. Without faith, we begin to fall into doubt, and from doubt we sink into fear. Fear leads to a breakdown of order and of spirit.

FAITH AND CREATIVITY

Faith is the fount of creativity. It is the medium through which the unmanifest becomes manifest. "In the beginning was the Word, and the Word was with God, and the Word was God. He was in the beginning with God; all things were made through him, and without him was not anything made that was made. . . . And the Word became flesh and dwelt among us, full of grace and truth" (Jn. 1:1–3, 14 RSV). The Word is Truth, and the fire of faith brings the flame of the everlasting, absolute Truth into manifestation in the world. We make flesh of the Truth by bringing it into the material realm. Faith, the substance unseen, transforms into the substance seen.

The astounding creativity of the human race would not be possible without faith. Throughout the ages, artists, inventors, scholars, and scientists have brought new things into being because of their vision—they could see the unseen, and they knew that it was obtainable. All progress happens because of faith.

Many times, visionaries are ridiculed by others who do not use their spiritual vision, who place their faith only upon what they can see with their physical eyes. In the early nineteenth century, the American engineer and inventor Robert Fulton saw with his faith-filled eyes that a boat could be propelled by steam. Others laughed and called him a fool. But Fulton persevered with his vision and created the steamboat. He made visible what he could see in the invisible realm of substance. People laughed at Henry Ford when he produced his first automobile and said it would never replace the horse. They scoffed at Christopher Latham Sholes when he (with others) created the typewriter in 1867. Similarly, the photocopying

XII
40
XXI

machine and the telephone were mocked as ideas with no practical value. When DeWitt Wallace conceived of the idea for a digest-sized magazine that would give people the highlights of the current media, giants in the publishing industry turned him away and urged him to abandon the idea. Wallace set up a publishing business in his garage in 1922. People predicted he would go bankrupt. But the little magazine caught on, because Wallace had seen the need for it with his faith-filled vision. Today, *Reader's Digest* is a multibillion-dollar, international publishing powerhouse.

Faith brings creativity into flower. But once we have the vision, we must act on it.

Faith and Spiritual Vision

While faith operates independently of spirituality, it is through spirituality that it soars to its heights. Faith, observed Charles Fillmore, is how we begin our religious experience. It quickens our spiritual understanding and opens spiritual discernment. Through faith, we can realize God. We become like Simon, Jesus' first disciple, whom he renamed Peter. The name *Simon* means "receptivity." When we begin our spiritual faith, we are receptive to the Word. As we quicken, we become like Peter, whose name means "faith." "On this rock I will build my church" (Mt. 16:18 RSV), said Jesus, referring to Peter and to the quality of "faith."

Jesus taught transformation of consciousness by word and by deed. He constantly admonished his disciples and audiences that belief and faith are key factors to that power. To illustrate this power, he performed numerous supernormal feats that were the products of his transformed consciousness: he was a superb healer; he manifested food; he changed water into wine; he raised the dead; he walked on water; he teleported his disciples; he was telepathic and knew the thoughts of others; he controlled the elements; he was transfigured into a body of radiant light. All of these things that he

did are also within our ability—if we but have faith. "He who believes in me will also do the works that I do; and greater works than
these will he do" (Jn. 14:12 RSV), said Jesus.

One of the most dramatic examples of what happens when we
doubt our faith occurred to Peter. Through faith, he began to walk
on water, as did Jesus. Yet when he became aware of the rough
wind and the turbulent waves, he became afraid, and his fear caused
him to sink. Peter cried out to Jesus to save him. Jesus reached out
his hand and caught him, saying, "O man of little faith, why did you
doubt?" (Mt. 14:31 RSV)

We find a similar story in Hinduism, as related by Sri Rama-
krishna:

> Once a man was about to cross the sea. Bibhishana wrote
> Rama's name [Prince Rama, an incarnation of God] on a
> leaf, tied it in a corner of the man's wearing-cloth, and said
> to him: "Don't be afraid. Have faith and walk on the water.
> But look here—the moment you lose faith you will be
> drowned." The man was walking easily on the water. Sud-
> denly he had an intense desire to see what was tied in his
> cloth. He opened it and found only a leaf with the name of
> Rama written on it. "What is this?" he thought. "Just the
> name of Rama!" As soon as doubt entered his mind he sank
> under the water.[2]

The men in both stories failed only when they turned their spiritual eye away from the invisible and focused on the visible—the
wind, the waves, a simple leaf with a name inscribed. If we put our
faith in what we see, we cannot manifest all the good that is ours.
If we say, "I'll believe it when I see it," we will always fall short of the
mark. Rather, we must say, "I believe, and therefore I see."

Jesus referred to the spiritual eye as "the lamp of the body." When
the eye is sound—that is, when it perceives the unseen and under-

stands the principle of faith—then the whole body is full of light. When our bodies are full of light, we are true channels for the divine power of God to flow through us, manifesting what the spiritual eye knows and sees through faith.

Fillmore placed this spiritual eye in the pineal gland in the center of the brain. This, he said, is the center of the power of faith and also the inner mind. Through prayer and meditation, we light up the inner mind. We receive wisdom and insight which we cannot put into words and which fuel our faith.

Faith gives us true spiritual vision. It is "the belief of the heart in that knowledge which comes from the Unseen," observed tenth-century Sufi mystic Muhammad B. Khafif. It enables us to see beyond the physical world into the world of potential and possibilities. There, all the good that is ours, and ours alone, awaits us. Faith helps us to see it, reach it, and create from it. We see the possible, even when tangible evidence in the material world tells us otherwise.

XII
—
43
—
XXI

FAITH AND PRAYER

"Faith and prayer go hand in hand," said Fillmore.[3] The language of prayer is based upon faith. Faith is assumed before we even begin our prayer. Without faith, prayer is unfocused, weak, and lackluster. Yet when we have faith, no matter what we say in prayer, God hears the faith and responds accordingly. The more we pray, the more our faith builds. Faith assures we will not "pray amiss," as the apostle James said concerning prayers that seem to go unanswered. All prayers are answered—in fact, they are answered in the moment we conceive them in the deepest parts of our hearts. The answers lie waiting for us before we even form the words in our minds or let them loose from our lips. When we have faith, we know that the answers are there for us, and we are confident that they will be revealed and we will receive what we need. The faith-filled prayer cannot go amiss.

But should we wait for faith before we pray? The answer is no. Even if we pray with seeds of doubts in our hearts or minds, the act of praying will erase those doubts. The smallest amount of faith will produce surprising results. Faith acts like a magnet. It draws to us that which we seek. We become filled with the substance unseen—the substance that connects us to our good.

One of the best and simplest ways we can strengthen our faith is to pray the names of God. Repeating a sacred name is a *mantra*. Literally, the term *mantra* means "to protect," especially the mind. According to Eastern mysticism, the mantra harnesses the power of the vibration of *shabda,* sacred sound. Repetition of mantras unleashes certain cosmic forces that drive deep into the consciousness. When we repeat the names of God, we are aligning every cell in our being with the highest consciousness possible. The constant repetition of holy vibrations raises up our own consciousness. We burst out into a new level of awareness and being, which becomes part of us without our having to think consciously about it. It functions like the hum of a generator.

Mantras are what Fillmore described as "faith words." Faith words are both formative and creative—formative, in that they bring things into being; creative, in that they tap into Divine Mind and "lay hold of Spirit substance and power." Faith words, according to Fillmore, should be said both silently and audibly.

All religions acknowledge the tremendous power of vibrating the names of God, either mentally or aloud. "God is love" or "I am one with God" are effective mantras. So is simply the name, "God." "Jesus Christ" and "Blessed Mother Mary" are also effective mantras. Remember the Indian man who sank when he found out he was carrying a leaf with "just the name of Rama" on it? In Hinduism, "Rama" is one of the most powerful and popular of mantras. In Sanskrit, it means "he who fills us with abiding joy."

Mantras help us to concentrate our mental forces, which in turn boosts the effectiveness of what we think. "The average thought vibration produces but temporary results," said Fillmore, "but under intense mind activity conditions more or less permanent are impressed upon the sensitive plate of the universal ether, and through this activity they are brought into physical manifestation."

What do we manifest by saying the names of God? The highest possible qualities are radiated back to us in a continuous stream. Unconditional love. Wholeness. Peace. Joy. Faith.

The beauty of the mantra is that for all its power, it requires little effort to put into practice. You do not have to set aside special time for it. You can repeat a mantra to yourself while you are doing virtually anything—driving the car, waiting in a line, doing chores around the house. "As you call upon His sacred name, do not entertain the faintest doubt of its efficacy," said Honen Shonin, twelfth-century founder of the Jodo school of Japanese Buddhism.

FAITH AND HEALING

Jesus performed healing more than any other deed. He healed instantly by touch. A mere word from him could heal. Even the sick who touched his clothing were healed. What made it possible? Faith.

Throughout his sermons and addresses, Jesus emphasized over and over again that faith is the pivotal factor. He grew exasperated when his disciples and also others could not grasp the simple idea that faith not only heals but also makes all things possible.

A man took his epileptic son to the disciples, but they could not heal him. So, the man appealed to Jesus. Jesus healed the boy instantly and said, "O faithless and perverse generation, how long am I to be with you? How long am I to bear with you?" When his disciples asked how he had been able to heal the boy when they had not, he said, "Because of your little faith. For truly, I say to you, if you have faith as a grain of mustard seed, you will say to this mountain, 'Move from here to there,' and it will move; and nothing will be impossible to you" (Mt. 17:17, 20–21 RSV).

A woman who had suffered for twelve years from hemorrhage believed that if she just touched the fringe of Jesus' garment, she would be healed. She did, and she was. "Take heart, daughter, your faith has made you well" (Mt. 9:22 RSV), Jesus said.

In the new era, our faith will lead us to more and more miracles of healing. We will believe in our own abilities to heal as Jesus did, and we will put them to use. Faith works through prayer, and prayer is the foundation of healing. The healing and prospering through faith in God is wonderfully demonstrated every minute of the day and night by the millions of calls and letters that pour in to Silent Unity, the international prayer ministry. The requests for prayer come from people around the world who have faith in the power of prayer to move mountains and to alleviate all afflictions.

Faith, Love, and Spiritual Community

Fillmore said that while we do not need religion to have faith, faith reaches its highest expression when we apply it to our spiritual lives. Faith is axiomatic to belief in God and to practicing a right and moral life. Jesus acknowledged that he did nothing by his own authority, but did everything only by the authority of God (Jn. 5:30 RSV). When we seek God, we understand that the same applies to us. We are in a dance of cocreation with the Divine to manifest what God wishes to bring into being. When we are in attunement with God, we manifest all that is whole and good. We bring the vibration of unconditional love into the world. When we are out of attunement, we allow ourselves to manifest discord and disharmony. Unconditional love and wholeness are the products of faith. Discord and disharmony are the products of fear.

A glance at the day's headlines shows that much of the world lives in the grip of fear. It does not have to be that way. We do not have to sink beneath the waves. We must make conscious choices to replace fear with faith and love. Faith works through love. Myrtle Fillmore said that "faith and love are qualities of Divine Mind that bring us into close communion with the Father and source of all light and blessings,"[4] and thus enable us to bring out the best in ourselves. Faith shines the light of love that dispels the darkness of fear.

Following faith instead of fear puts us firmly onto a spiritual path. When we follow a spiritual path, we place God first. In placing God first, we have faith that our needs will be met. "Do not be anxious about your life, what you shall eat or what you shall drink, nor about your body, what you shall put on . . ." said Jesus. "Look at the birds of the air: they neither sow nor reap nor gather into barns, and yet your heavenly Father feeds them" (Mt. 6:25-26 RSV).

We derive much support and nourishment from being part of a spiritual community. By gathering together with like-minded individuals to pray, heal, and worship, we accelerate the process of spiritual growth, not only for ourselves but also for all persons. In the new era, having the anchor of spiritual church and community will facilitate the process of transformation of the soul.

We are beginning to truly understand and appreciate that we are all connected, that we are all part of a whole. New physics teaches us what mystics have known for millennia: that ultimately everything is connected in a unified field and that the natural drift of the universe is toward wholeness. In Hinduism, we find the story of Indra's net. Indra, the god of the firmament, has a huge net. Everything in creation hangs on this net as jewels. If one jewel shakes, the entire net and all the jewels shake. We are learning as never before that what we think, what we believe, and what we do shake the entire net of creation.

When we come together in spiritual community, we create a synergistic effect, in which the group consciousness becomes more than the sum of its individual parts. We find a basis for this in the Bible, especially related to prayer, in the words of Jesus: "For where two or three are gathered in my name, there am I in the midst of them" (Mt. 18:20 RSV).

Community can help us sharpen our spiritual vision and strengthen our faith.

How Are We to Use Faith?

Despite the mountains of evidence that faith enables us to work wonders, we don't put faith to its full use. Rather than develop our spiritual muscles through prayer, meditation, right thinking, right living, and dreaming big goals, we wait for catastrophe to strike. Then we beseech God for help, hoping that God will come through quickly, but feeling panic that our prayers might not work. How foolish! Had we practiced our faith every day, we would know without doubt that every prayer is answered.

Even without catastrophe, we sometimes doubt our faith. We set a goal and then wonder if we will reach it. Doubt creeps into our minds about our skills and abilities. Every time even the tiniest doubt enters our minds, we erode faith and thus erode our ability to achieve the heights.

Because of our doubts, we ask for signs of assurance, proof that prayers are answered, that God exists, that God works through humanity, that we can do what we think we can do. We say, "If only I can have a sign, then I will have faith." But if we have faith in the first place, we do not need the signs and proofs. With faith, we know that life itself is an ongoing proof of the covenant of God. We know that we will be provided for. We know that every problem will find a solution. We know that we will succeed. We know that we can work miracles.

We also do not use our full miracle-manifesting potential, because it is characteristic of people to let others do their thinking for them. We give our power away. We think that only certain appointed ones, certain mystics or prophets or institutions, can access the power of Spirit. This is erroneous thinking, and it keeps us away from our good and from realizing our full potential. We all have access to the same substance, the same power. We must believe that we do. We must have faith that we do. In so believing, we have it in an instant.

We must open our eyes to the fact that we are all mystics, prophets, and healers. We always have been—we have simply given those powers away to others. Part of Jesus' divine mission was to be the Wayshower to awaken us to our potential. His disciples awakened and performed miraculous acts of their own. But in the ensuing centuries, we became complacent. Our faith wavered, and we did not follow suit.

Now is the time to claim our powers. The institutions that have looked after us in the past—governmental, social, educational, health—are strained beyond their capacities. Every day we read about cutbacks and the inability to sustain services. We can no longer depend on institutions to solve our problems. The betterment of society, and thus of the collective human spiritual condition, is depending increasingly on each and every individual. We must awaken our powers without delay. That is why faith has become like a fire. It fuels our passion, galvanizes us to make change.

Myrtle Fillmore emphasized over and over again how we should use faith: "Have faith in yourself." [5]

FAITH AND THE EVOLVING SOUL

Our consciousness is on an evolutionary track. Even the ancients realized this; the Greeks, for example, envisioned ladders of cleansing and advancement of the soul. In more recent times, numerous scenarios have been put forward by philosophers and scientists, in which humanity advances by gradual, spiraling evolution punctuated by abrupt minor steps and major leaps forward. The works of Pierre Teilhard de Chardin, G. Ledyard Stebbins, Michael Grosso,

Peter Russell, Kenneth Ring, Gopi Krishna, and Michael Murphy are but a few in this arena. Futurists generally agree that the pace of evolution is increasing as the creativity of our self-reflective consciousness begets more creativity. "We now appear to be in the midst of an unprecedented period of extremely rapid development," notes futurist Peter Russell.[6]

Major leaps open the way for evolutionary transcendence, a new order of existence. The emergence of life from inorganic matter was one such transcendent leap, and the development of consciousness another. Future transcendent leaps will depend on the collective consciousness as we realize that our beliefs, thoughts, and projections of will do create and shape our reality and as we also learn that we are inseparably part of a whole pattern. Our own self-reflective consciousness is leading an accelerating evolution—an inner evolution as well as an external one. "Thus the urge that many people feel to grow and develop inwardly may well be the force of evolution manifesting within our own consciousnesses," says Russell. "It is the universe evolving through us."[7]

The universe evolving through us is the expression of God through the works of humanity. Scientists have long held that we use but a fraction of our brain and have speculated on the possibilities if we could use more of our natural assets. We are already tapping into these assets, bringing about extraordinary changes.

Futurist Michael Murphy outlines twelve sets of human attributes that will characterize the new epochal transition for humanity: (1) extraordinary perceptions in the form of psi; (2) extraordinary somatic awareness and self-regulation; (3) extraordinary communication abilities, such as telepathy and ecstatic states; (4) super-abundant vitality beyond ordinary body processes; (5) extraordinary movement abilities; (6) extraordinary capacities to alter the environment, such as through psychokinesis; (7) self-existent delight; (8) supreme intellectual capacities and abilities characteristic of genius; (9) volition exceeding ordinary will, producing extraordinary actions; (10) transcendent personhood; (11) transcendent love; and (12) "alterations in bodily structures, states, and processes that support the experiences and capacities just noted."[8]

Many of these are abilities that in times past we would have labeled miraculous. In fact, they are the same abilities demonstrated by Jesus. We must change our thinking about what is "miraculous," as though a miracle were beyond our ken. Our evolution is being driven by the state of our consciousness—our awareness of our own potential and our faith in our ability to manifest it. The key to this evolution is faith. In order to advance, we have to make the conscious choice to do so. We have to believe in our own potential.

We shall all work miracles. We shall all do the works that Jesus did—those things and greater, as he predicted. In the new era, faith is more important than ever. When we truly put our faith to work, miracles will be the norm, rather than the exception. We will learn to go beyond the realm of intellect and information. We have more information at our fingertips than at any other time in the history of the human race, and yet information will not help us manifest miracles. Faith will. Charles Fillmore said that "intellectual people do no miracles through faith, because they always limit its scope to what the intellect says is law."[9] Faith must be exercised deep within spiritual consciousness for miracles to flow forth.

MASTERY OF LIFE

Faith in the new era is a faith of mastery. Through faith, we rise above the ordinary and become masters of our lives. We know we are the living embodiments of God. Bolstered by the spiritual fires of community, we are empowered to reach any goals. Be a master of life. Believe now that the Creator endowed you with miracle-making abilities. Believe now that you are filled with the radiance of transcendent love. Believe now that your spiritual lamp shines on the path ahead, illuminating a universe of unlimited potential. Go forward. Faith will be your unerring guide.

Rosemary Ellen Guiley is the best-selling author of numerous books delving into exceptional human experience—those events and insights that push out the frontiers of our understanding of the nature of the human soul and consciousness. Her books include the following: *The Miracle of Prayer: True Stories of Blessed Healings; Blessings: Prayers for the Home and Family; The Encyclopedia of Dreams: Symbols and Interpretations; The Encyclopedia of Angels;* and *Angels of Mercy.* Her latest book is *Prayer Works: True Stories of Answered Prayer.*

Rosemary serves on the board of trustees of the Academy of Religion and Psychical Research, the academic affiliate of the Spiritual Frontiers Fellowship International. She is an Honorary Fellow of the College of Human Sciences, the professional membership division of the International Institute of Integral Human Sciences in Montreal, a nonprofit organization affiliated with the United Nations. She presents lectures and workshops internationally and appears on radio and television. She has been featured on The Discovery Channel, The Learning Channel, and in the *Time-Life* video series.

XII

52

XXI

CHAPTER III

THE POWER OF
UNDERSTANDING

Left all to itself, faith can tend to become foolishly blind. It would be as if Peter attempted to build the church entirely by himself. Would it not be a temple to one man's ego, to one man's limitations? We have all met people who practice their faith in rigid, narrow ways.

The powers are meant to travel together and work together. The power of understanding, represented by the disciple Thomas, flows well with faith. Understanding is the left-brain, intellectual, questioning, probing, sometimes doubtful part of our mind. When Thomas doubted Jesus' identity when he appeared after his resurrection, Jesus respected Thomas' demand for proof.

By beginning the process of proper discernment, understanding develops wisdom. Understanding brings to the heartful, open, perceiving power of faith a capacity to be broadminded, inclusive, and generous. Faith brings to the intellectual side of understanding a deeper, more selfless, more compassionate way of being. Together, "understanding faith" is a strong foundation on which to build a ministry, a life, a world.

Understanding: Acceleration in Spiritual Information

Sir John Marks Templeton

For more than seventy-five years, I have been reading the works of Unity School of Christianity, especially the writings of Charles, Myrtle, and Lowell Fillmore. The Unity School viewpoint is especially attractive because of its willingness to be open and receptive and non-opposing to the writings of other denominations and religions. A desire to increase in understanding speaks of a humility of spirit that can mean serving others, as when Jesus said, "Whoever would be great among you must be your servant" (Mt. 20:26 RSV). Charles Fillmore taught that "Spiritual discernment reveals that knowledge and intelligence are auxiliary to understanding."[1] Understanding can both spring from and produce an inner feeling for right relations. It enhances the ability to lay hold of right relationships and utilize them for the highest good of humanity—a quality so pertinent at this moment in history.

Presently, we stand poised on the brink of another new century—indeed, a new millennium. We are perched on the frontiers of future knowledge. We live in a wonderful age, a period of unprecedented discovery and opportunity, a blossoming time for mankind. It is also a world of dramatic changes—politically, economically, culturally, philosophically, scientifically, and spiritually. The evolution of human knowledge is accelerating enormously.

More than half of the scientists who ever lived are alive today. More than half of the discoveries in the natural sciences have been made in this century. More than half of the goods produced in the history of the earth have been produced since 1800. More than half the books ever written were written in the last fifty years. More new books are published each month than were written in the entire historical period before Columbus!

Even though we stand upon the enormous mountain of information collected over recent centuries of scientific progress, we have only fleeting glimpses of the future. To a large extent, the future lies before us like a vast wilderness of unexplored reality. The God who created and sustains the evolving universe through eons of progress and development may not have placed us at the tag end of the creative process. We may be at a new beginning. We may be here for the future!

Our role is crucial. As human beings, we are endowed with mind and spirit. We can think, imagine, and dream. We can search for future trends through the rich diversity of human thought. God permits us in some ways to be cocreators with Him in the continuing act of creation. We know, in a vast and intricate cosmos, that there is still much more to be discovered. We need to understand, and we need to plan! With the sheer driving force of advancing technology, it becomes increasingly clear that our society is moving from a material-based one to an information-oriented and knowledge-intensive base.

Today, most Americans spend their time creating, processing, or distributing information. One distinction of the information economy is that it is based upon renewable and self-generating resources—knowledge and information—and a need for greater understanding of both! The explosion of international trade, communications, and information increasingly influences the way we live, bringing about global lifestyles. Let's take a brief look at just a few of the many facts—economically, medically, technologically, educationally, and spiritually—that seem to be affecting the accelerating pace of progress.

Economic Facts

We live in a period of prosperity such as never seen before in the world's history. The American gross national product is over thirty times what it was just fifty years ago. The average hourly wage of a factory worker has increased in real terms by over 65 percent. Private net worth has increased fivefold, after adjusting for inflation, within the past fifty years. America has over one million millionaires, and there are over two hundred billionaires worldwide! Not only do we earn more, but our quality of life has also increased. Within my lifetime, the real consumption per person worldwide has more than quadrupled! It is the first time that such quadrupling in the standard of living has occurred in the span of a single person's lifetime.

In seeking to understand what is happening, recent work by a Yale University economist suggests that researchers may have understated real wage growth by failing to account for qualitative improvements in goods and services. Adjusting for quality improvements means that the standard of living in America may have increased by a factor of seventy-five times since 1800! Even conventional measures suggest it has increased by thirteen times, which is still a tremendous amount.

Expanding our view around the world, the growth that has taken place in just this century has been equally impressive. Today, people worldwide consume 20 percent more food per person than just fifty years ago. The number of people playing sports has increased ten times within the last century. People benefit buying more than one hundred times as much energy as they did only a century earlier. Just in the past thirty years, improvements in crop varieties, pesticides, and fertilizers have helped triple agricultural production per acre. Without these changes, we would have had to clear forests from an area about the size of North America just for more farming! Underlying this growth is the increasing acceptance of the importance of free trade and enterprise within and among nations, which certainly requires clearer communication and understanding among people.

MEDICAL FACTS

Remarkable advances have been witnessed in all areas and around the world. For example, in the field of medicine, death from tuberculosis, typhoid fever, diphtheria, syphilis, pneumonia, and diabetes is now only a tiny fraction of what it was fifty years ago. Miscarriages have been cut in half, as has the number of infants who die in the first year of life. Doctors, research scientists, and technicians in the medical field are gleaning greater understanding of the human body and how it works and finding new technologies that pave the way for increased good health and longevity.

Even in areas where we still face significant bodily challenges, we can be encouraged by progress that is being made. In the 1930s, the five-year survival rate for cancer patients was 20 percent. Today, it is better than 50 percent!

Over the last fifty years, the number of physicians licensed in America has tripled. And many say that 50 percent of today's medical knowledge has been discovered in the last 15 years, with over 90 percent being discovered during the present century! When we realize that over half of all the research scientists who ever lived are alive today, we can see that this incredible pace of advancement is likely to continue into the future.

TECHNOLOGICAL FACTS

Technology and communications are other areas which have seen unparalleled growth. Today, eight times as much is spent on video and audio equipment and personal computers as was spent just twenty-five years ago. The percentage of American households with telephones has doubled within the past fifty years. New fiber-optic lines can carry eight thousand conversations, as compared to forty-eight on the old copper wire.

Just think: Fifty years ago there were no computers, Xeroxes, lasers, microchips, man-made satellites, fax machines, modems, interstate highways, cassette recorders, or cellular phones! As amazing as these inventions are, it is even more amazing how quickly many of them are becoming obsolete. Take the microchip, for example. It is estimated that the power of the microchip doubles every eighteen months! This means that computers built ten years from now could be seventy times more powerful!

As communications and travel have grown, so have new ideas and inventions. From the time of Jesus to the mid-eighteenth century, history states that knowledge doubled. It had doubled again one hundred fifty years later, and then again in only fifty years! Incredibly, more new information has been produced within the last thirty years than was produced in the previous five thousand years!

Progress of this magnitude in such a short period of time is truly a revolution, one whose astounding implications have yet to be fully understood. When the telephone was first introduced, a British leader commented that while it was fine for the United States, it would not be needed in England, which was small and had many messenger boys!

I believe one of the most significant implications of this information revolution lies in its seemingly infinite nature. Our economic prosperity is no longer primarily a function of limited natural resources, but is becoming progressively more heavily dependent on the self-perpetuating, limitless body of knowledge. We have traditionally thought of wealth in terms of tangible things like gold or land. Increasingly, wealth has become intangibly rooted in knowledge and its application through greater understanding.

EDUCATIONAL OPPORTUNITIES

The explosion in both the volume and the rate at which information is available, combined with the greater level of prosperity that already exists, has afforded more and more people the opportunity to learn. A progressively higher level of learning will become an essential part of this ongoing transformation that can enhance the future course of nearly every field of study and line of work. It is important to develop the analytical skills necessary to harness the powers of knowledge with understanding to drive the engine of future economic growth.

The level of education is improving around the globe. In America, nearly three-fourths of all seventeen-year-olds graduate from high school today, as compared with 50 percent just fifty years ago. There are twice as many institutions of higher education for them to attend. Five times as many earn their bachelor's degrees and eleven times as many continue their studies to receive master's degrees or doctorates. In China, the literacy rate has increased from under 20 percent in 1950 to over 60 percent today. In Indonesia, the literacy rate has grown from 9 percent in 1930 to over sixty percent also. This same story is spreading throughout the developing world. Worldwide, the percentage of children enrolled in secondary education has more than doubled, going from 31 percent to over 65 percent since 1970!

The more we are able to take advantage of the information explosion around us and the more we are able to liberate our minds from routine tasks and cultivate high degrees of analytical thinking, the greater the prosperity with which we will be rewarded.

RELIGIOUS FACTS

During my lifetime, natural scientists have studied spiritual matters as never before. The Templeton Foundation Prize for Progress in Religion focuses attention on people who are doing new and original thinking in religion. The prize was first awarded to the late Mother Teresa of Calcutta in 1973. It has been given to religious leaders across the entire spectrum of belief, from the late Sir Sarvepalli Radhakrishnan, a President of India, to Protestant evangelist Billy Graham. The particular nature of the prize, which carries with it a cash award, reflects my perspective that spiritual development is more important than progress in all the other fields combined!

It is tremendously encouraging that there are many new organizations involved in the field of progress in religion, such as the American Scientific Affiliation, The Christian Medical Society, Christians in Science, The International Academy of Religious Sciences, The Center for Advanced Study in Religion and Sciences, the Humility Theology Information Center, and the Center of Theological Inquiry.

This century has also witnessed the formation of the World Council of Churches, the Friends Service Committee, The American Association of Theological Schools, The National Association of Evangelicals, Church World Service, Campus Crusade, World of Life, Youth of Christ, The Fellowship of Christian Athletes, Intervarsity Fellowship, Youth Life, Pentecostal World Conference, *The Zygon Journal,* and the Christian Businessmen's Fellowship.

Additional spiritual research organizations are being formed almost every year. Can you imagine the quantum leap forward that could occur if at least one-tenth as much money were spent on spiritual research as is spent on scientific research? This would amount to $100 million every day! How little we know, and how eager we are to learn! It is time to take a step in this direction, and the Templeton Foundation plans to spend over $30 million each year in the twenty-first century encouraging progress in spiritual information and research!

We are truly blessed to have been a part of the remarkable progress that has occurred in such a short time. Change is rarely smooth and painless. Setbacks and disappointments often occur along the way. Unfortunately, too often we tend to focus on the negative aspects and lose sight of the multitude of blessings which surround us and the limitless potential which exists for the future. God's children on earth have been given free will and creativity and purpose. It appears that God wants humans to participate in His ongoing creative purposes.

The underlying premise in my personal theology is that to make progress toward a fuller understanding of God, man must be "humble" before the divine presence. Humility is a key to progress. Without it, we can become too self-satisfied with past glories to launch boldly into the challenges ahead. Without humility, we may not be wide-eyed and open-minded enough to discover new areas for research. If we do not become as humble as children, we may be unable to admit mistakes, seek advice, desire understanding, and try again. The humble approach is for all of us who are concerned about the future of our civilization and the role we are to play in it. It is a receptive approach for all of us who are not satisfied to let things drift and who want to channel our creative restlessness toward helping to build the kingdom of God. I often reflect on these words of Albert Einstein: "The most wonderful thing we can experience is the mysterious. It is the source of all art and science. He to whom this emotion is a stranger, who can no longer pause to wonder and stand rapt in awe, is as good as dead; his eyes are closed."

In humility, we can learn from each other, for it opens us up. We become receptive to seeing things from the other person's point of view, and we can share ours with him or her freely. We can begin to see significant elements of truth in all situations. We desire right relations in our interactions with others, and we can avoid the sins of pride, intolerance, and strife by being willing to be more understanding. Humility opens the door to the realms of the Spirit and to research and progress in religion.

A story is told of a man who was ill. His money was rapidly disappearing in medical bills, and his condition did not seem to be improving. He prayed for three things that seemed most important to him. First, he asked for the patience to handle his condition of illness. Next, he prayed for enough money to pay his bills. Third, he prayed for healing. As he held these thoughts in meditation, the man suddenly realized why his prayers were not working. How could he be healed if he was so intent in developing the patience and funds to cover *continued* illness? The man finally realized that he was putting the cart before the horse. He actually had only one authentic need, which was to open his mind to a realization of the One. He prayed for humility and understanding! The man found health and also happiness.

THE PHILOSOPHICAL SEARCH FOR UNDERSTANDING

It has been said, philosophically, that earth is a school. If this is correct, who are the teachers? If we take a close look at our world, one teacher could be called adversity. Then we might ask, why did God put souls into a world of tribulations? Why did not the Creator of all there is just make souls perfect in the first place? Is not God vastly more farsighted and infinitely wiser than we are? Perhaps from God's perspective the sorrows and tribulations of this earth are the best way to educate souls.

Growth can come through trial and self-discipline. Found in learning and understanding the laws of life is a wealth of evidence that indicates spiritual growth and happiness come from learning to give, rather than from "getting." God has given us free will for new interpretations and understanding of eternal Truths, so that in our limited way we can be creative. Of course, free will also gives us the awesome power to build our own individual hells and heavens here on earth. Out of our desire to change the world for the better, we learn that the principle of creation is change and that through change will God's creativity continue.

For there to be progress, there should be a set of standards to follow, a goal to shoot for, a set of ultimate values to affirm. Otherwise, the upward movement that constitutes human progress becomes random, aimless motion. And the human dramas that make up the events of our daily lives, as they are grouped in larger expanses of historical periods, become meaningless babel, with no discernible order or structure.

For there to be progress, there should be underlying understandings about what constitutes progress. It's at this point that spiritual progress joins hands with other kinds of progress and contributes ultimate meaning and direction to the entire creative process. Spiritual progress has both inner and outer dimensions that promote personal and social improvement. Spiritual progress involves something that is new. And spiritual progress often includes, or is combined with, progress in other fields of endeavor. For example, new ways of helping the poor and underprivileged in our world may be to help donees to become donors.

This is the blossoming time in the creation of humanity. Evolution is accelerating; progress is accelerating. One of God's great blessings to humanity is change, and the present escalation of change in the world is an overflowing of this blessing. The world urgently needs new breakthroughs for our basic understandings of God. Every person's concept of God is too small. Through humility, we can begin to get into true perspective the infinity of God. This is the humble approach (and it may be a science still in its infancy), but it seeks to develop a way of knowing God appropriate to His greatness and our littleness. It is a search which looks forward, not backward, and which expects to learn and grow in understanding from its mistakes. Are we ready to begin the formulation of a humble theology that can never become obsolete?

This would be a theology really centered on God and not our own little selves.

SCIENCE AND RELIGION

If laws of the Spirit are fragments of knowledge about God, so also, in their way, are the laws of nature. It is important to honor scientists who are committed to studying the divine as it manifests itself in the physical world. If courses were offered on topics related to theology through science, cosmology, and experimentation, we might be in for some surprising discoveries!

We might reaffirm what Henry Drummond discovered in the 1850s; namely, that the supernatural is more natural than strange. He suggested:

> What is required to draw Science and Religion together again—for they began the centuries hand in hand—is the disclosure of the naturalness of the supernatural. Then, and not until then, will men see how true it is, that to be loyal to all of Nature, they must be loyal to the part defined as spiritual. . . . And even as the contribution of Science to Religion is the vindication of the naturalness of the Supernatural, so the gift of Religion to Science is the demonstration of the supernaturalness of the Natural. Thus, as the Supernatural become slowly Natural, will also the Natural become slowly Supernatural, until in the impersonal authority of Law men everywhere recognize the Authority of God.

If Drummond was correct, we may find that members of both the scientific and religious communities have a common base from which to speak to each other. Scientists have steadily been changing their concepts of the universe and laws of nature, but the progres-

XII
—
64
—
XXI

sion is away from smaller, self-centered, or human-centered concepts. Evidence is always accumulating that things seen are only one aspect of the vastly greater, unseen realities. Human observational abilities are very limited, and so are our mental abilities. Should we not focus on the unseen realities instead of the fleeting appearances?

Not only is faith a common element in the experience of different nationalities and cultures throughout history, and of a cross section of economic and educational groups in contemporary society, but it also has a profound involvement in the practice of science. The reason for the success of the scientific enterprise was, in the view of philosopher-scientist Walter Thorson, traceable to these theological roots. Scientists were taking God's creation seriously, in a way neglected by the medieval church. The truth about the physical world was not only fascinating to explore, but, in the view of these devout people, a valid indication of genuine reality. If some theologians of the period regarded the physical world as only a kind of papier-mâché prop for the playing out of the drama of salvation, some believing scientists saw it instead as a valid source of blessing, with its own integrity and spiritual opportunity. Here was evidence to be explored in an effort to fully appreciate the Divine Artist's handiwork.

If you stand on a sidewalk, you may not see the beginning or the end of it. In fact, it seems endless. But if somehow you can reach a vantage point well above the sidewalk, you can see all its configurations as it stretches out in front of you and behind you. You can see where it begins and ends, what's beyond it and around it, and how the different sections of the sidewalk relate to one another in the context of the whole. But only a little of this "divine" perspective is available to your sight when you are planted on the ground.

Two factors are especially important in the effort to achieve progress in any field, including both religion and science. One is the ability to ask the right kind of provocative questions. The other is the establishment of open forums of discussion, so that researchers from a variety of backgrounds can present their findings and hone them to a sharp edge in informed debate.

A HUMILITY THEOLOGY INFORMATION CENTER

The John Templeton Foundation has established as one of its primary goals the promotion of a greater awareness among thinking people—especially scientists and theologians—of the vast magnitude of the Creator, God, and the enormity of our own ignorance. The attitude of humility that such an awareness promotes might have profound impact upon the goals of both scientists and theologians. There could be fresh openness to spiritual dimensions—with scientists focusing more of their energies on research into spiritual information and with theologians contributing fresh interpretations and new directions of theological explanation.

The increasing appreciation of the vastness and intricacy of the universe and the subtlety of its interrelationships, which science is beginning to reveal, carries with it profound theological implications. This new theological outlook is part of the theology of humility. For this purpose, the foundation is planning a Humility Theology Information Center. The Center's focus includes the following areas of concentration:

- Utilization of scientific methods in understanding the work and purpose of the Creator.
- Research relative to studying or stimulating progress in spirituality.
- Research relative to the benefits of religion.

The possibilities from addressing these and many other questions could be vastly illuminating. Thousands of religions are gone and forgotten because they ossified by the concept of "we know it all." Throughout history, many religions have become obsolete and died because they were stagnant, rather than progressive. If you know it all already, you have little desire to learn more; but if no human has ever known even 1 percent of the infinity of God, then you may have a burning desire to help with new discoveries.

Perhaps, unawakened humanity is like a wave on the ocean and God is like the ocean. Maybe the limited human soul is like a molecule in a wave. Should the molecule try to prove that the ocean exists? Or vice versa? Could the search for evidence of purpose be more fruitful than the search for evidence of life? Could an evolution devoid of purpose create humans dominated by purpose? Increased understanding in cosmology shows that the universe is more than a billion billion times larger than anyone imagined a few centuries ago.

The Theology of Humility means that we know so little and need to learn and understand so much, in addition to devoting resources to research. This area of study is not man-centered, but God-centered. It proposes that the infinite God may not even be describable adequately in human words and concepts and may not be limited by human rationality.

A main purpose of the John Templeton Foundation is to encourage the top .1 percent of people (and, thereby, suggest to all people) to think that progress in spiritual information is possible and desirable—that it can and will be done. As in other sciences, the benefits are often unforeseen. More and more information (if verified by statistical or experimental evidence or other methods of science) can be recognized worldwide promptly after each discovery and, thereby, provide an increasing supplement to the wonderful revelations of all ancient scriptures and prophets, which have been so beneficial for thousands of years.

The Theology of Humility interprets modern scientific developments in regard to understanding what they might reveal about spiritual principles and the nature and ways of God. In addition, where appropriate, it seeks to apply the hypothetical deductive methods of the sciences to experimentation with spiritual data. Often this can be done by posing concepts in a testable mode, reflecting the provisionality, incompleteness, and fallibility of human utterances about spiritual reality.

The Theology of Humility begins with the assumption that, because of our finitude in the face of the vastness of all reality, human knowledge about God and about the world the scientist explores should be regarded as very limited and tentatively held. Toward this end, it encourages an open-mindedness toward any new ideas, a respectful manner of engagement with those who hold different views, and a nondogmatic style of presenting ideas. Humility Theology encourages an attitude of respect among theologians and scientists for all religious traditions; openness to new theological insights based on the broadest possible range of human learning, testing, and experience; and reverence toward God as the unlimited creative spirit and ultimate reality. The Theology of Humility suggests that tremendous benefits could accrue from our greater understanding of spiritual subjects, such as love, prayer, meditation, thanksgiving, giving, forgiving, and surrender to the divine will. It further suggests that since science is opening our eyes to the vast works of an infinite Creator, science may also be applied to varieties of experimental and statistical studies of these spiritual entities. It may be that we shall see the beginning of a new age of "experimental theology," wherein studies may reveal there are spiritual laws, universal principles which operate in the spiritual domain, just as some natural laws function in the tangible realm. Perhaps we may discover that the sphere of Spirit is intensifying as God's evolving plans unfold and accelerate.

PROGRESS IN SPIRITUAL UNDERSTANDING

In only one century, understanding may have increased more than one-hundredfold in medicine, electronics, communications, and biology. Maybe in the twenty-first century humans can expand their understanding of spiritual information to more than tenfold. From medical research we now know more than one hundred times as much about our body as was known only a century ago. But how much more do we know about the soul? Maybe the twenty-first century could go down in history for the acceleration of progress in spiritual understanding.

At this moment in time, scientists, philosophers, theologians, laity—all of us—should utilize greater understanding of such current world views in our continuing participation in creation. Admitting we might be proven wrong, we launch boldly into new discoveries. And what new discoveries are to be made? To think that man on this planet is the end of evolution would be egotistical and anthropocentric indeed. It has always been difficult to imagine what comes next, but the multitude of discoveries in this century of things previously unseen points towards the likelihood of even more amazing discoveries hereafter.

How astounding it is that after billions of years of evolution of the earth had taken place, a new creation, a new *kind* of evolution, could suddenly burst forth! The dramatic change was the appearance of man, a creature with free will—the first creature on earth to be allowed to participate in the creative process. Until then, evolution seemed to follow a course fixed by laws of nature. Now, suddenly, the inconceivable has happened: self-evolution, intentional evolution, has begun. The earth is filled with creations of a new kind—logic, love, understanding, mathematics, worship, purpose, inventions, and multitudes of other creations never seen on earth before. In reality, after four billion years of earthly evolution, a new world has been born—a world of mind! The appearance of humankind on this planet may be said to have heralded the coming of a new quality encircling the earth—the sphere of the intellect. Then as we have used our intellects to investigate this mysterious universe, accumulating knowledge at an ever-increasing rate, there has come a growing awareness that material things are not what they seem, that maybe thoughts are more real and lasting than matter and energy!

Perhaps this heralds a new quality, the sphere of Spirit. God may be creating not only the infinitely large, but also the infinitely small; not only the outward, but also the inward; not only the tangible, but also the intangible. Thoughts, mind, soul, wisdom, love, originality, inspiration, and enthusiasm may be little manifestations of a Creator who is omniscient, omnipotent, timeless, and unbounded. The things that we see, hear, and touch may be only appearances. They may be only manifestations of underlying forces, including spiritual forces that may persist throughout all the transience of physical existence. Perhaps the spiritual world, and the benevolent Creator whom it reflects, may be true reality.

All in all, the voices for the millennium will certainly be calling for greater understanding in all areas of human endeavors—scientifically, philosophically, and spiritually. This will be the kind of awareness that can incorporate increasingly modern scientific discoveries into a higher, more fundamental understanding of the cosmos.

Sir John Marks Templeton is one of the great legends of the business world. Some years ago, at the age of 79, he retired from his investment company, sold it for some $400 million, and devoted himself to making the world a better place.

In 1973 The Templeton Foundation Prize for Progress in Religion was founded to encourage research in religion the way the Nobel prize rewards advances in the sciences. The $1,250,000 prize is given yearly to an individual who advances public understanding of God, or spirituality.

John Templeton was a Rhodes scholar at Oxford and earned a degree in economics at Yale. He has long been known for his wise mutual fund investment advice and for his optimistic vision of America's future. He is the author of *Discovering the Laws of Life* and *Worldwide Laws of Life*.

CHAPTER IV

THE POWER OF WISDOM

"Happy are those who find wisdom,
    and those who get understanding,
for her income is better than silver,
    and her revenue better than gold.
She is more precious than jewels,
    and nothing you desire can compare with her.
Long life is in her right hand;
    in her left hand are riches and honor.
Her ways are ways of pleasantness,
    and all her paths are peace.
She is a tree of life to those who lay hold of her;
    those who hold her fast are called happy.
The Lord by wisdom founded the earth;
    by understanding he established the heavens."*
                       —Proverbs 3:13–19

Wisdom, represented by the disciple James of Zebedee—"James the Just," brother of John—is the partnership of love, faith, and understanding. You could say that love is the offspring of faith and understanding—and wisdom grows up in their household. Wisdom has both faith and understanding in it, for it provides love with discernment, the spiritual discrimination or judgment that separates the wheat from the chaff, the true from the false. Those who hold fast to wisdom, we call "happy."

71

The Age of Wisdom

Eric Butterworth

We are living in one of the most exciting times of history, and if we are observant, we can say, "It's great to be alive." Nations around the world are breaking their bonds of oppression and experiencing true freedom. It is a beautiful thing to see. For fifty years, human bondage was symbolized by the Berlin Wall. And now the razing of the wall has become a symbol of the walls of separation that are dissolving for great masses of people.

In this new experience of human freedom, there is a widespread hunger for Truth and a search for reality and meaning. This search is normally thought to be on the pathway of religion. We tend to think of religion as an organization we join, the custom-made convictions we accept, or the church we stay away from. However, in our use of the word *religion*, we are thinking not about institutions or theologies, but about a transcendent perspective on life.

Arnold Toynbee observes that a great challenge facing mankind today is the challenge to traditional religion to find a present-day faith that corresponds to present-day needs—in other words, religion that is practical.

The twentieth century has been the era of New Thought in America. A University of Chicago survey indicated that more than two-thirds of all Americans already believe in at least some aspect of what one writer calls, "New Thought–New Age–metaphysical-occultism" as taught by Unity. This wave of believing energy I call "the new insight in Truth" may be coalescing into a "millennial theology" that some think will be the religion of the third millennium.

An article in the *Atlantic Monthly* some years ago called attention to the fact that there was a profound desire for religion in the world which no church or sect seemed to be satisfying. The article closed with the question of whether any existing church has the energy to free itself from its own past, to proclaim the Truth that Christianity is yet to be discovered and practiced. It said, "If not, we may dare to predict that a new church will arise and destroy the old ones."

This is not to claim that the "millennial theology" articulated by the New Thought-New Age teachings is this "new church," or to agree that the old ones must be destroyed. It is obvious, however, that these modern metaphysical teachings have come into being as a direct result of the failure of the traditional church to realize that "Christianity is yet to be discovered."

Professor Toynbee concluded from his monumental lifelong study of history that a religious resurgence (but not a revival of current religions) would be vital to the survival of Western civilization. It is my hope and prayer that this book may contribute to such a resurgence.

For one who has a compelling need to know "what makes things tick," this is an exciting time to be alive. Who could then have imagined that the young lad picking up a broadcasting signal on his primitive "crystal set" would one day experience our electronic communications revolution? And who could have imagined the "information explosion" by which we have come to know more about the Universe in the past seventy-five years than in all the history of civilization preceding that time. And today my little grandson has his "crystal set" in the form of a personal computer with a modem. And he matter-of-factly launches out on the Internet with a world of vast pools of information at his disposal.

We could characterize the times as "The Age of Wisdom." However, as a society we may become so bedazzled with the amazing flow of information, that we confuse education with the accumulation and correlation of facts. I often say to a class that learning is what remains when we have forgotten all we have heard in the day's teaching process.

Immanuel Kant says, "Science is organized knowledge. Wisdom is organized life." We are wise only if we can correlate our knowledge into consciousness whereby it improves the true level of our lives and enables us to help others do the same.

ROLE OF SCRIPTURE

This also has obvious implications in knowledge about Jesus or the Bible and, for that matter, knowledge about Truth. Christian fundamentalist preachers make emotional appeals to people to study the Scriptures, and thus Bible classes abound. It is a rote learning process, accepting a meticulously literal reading of the Bible. Students are judged on the quantity of Scripture they can parrot. Conveniently omitted from this "quantity," is Jesus' clear instruction in John 5:39–40 (ASV): "Ye search the scriptures, because ye think that in them ye have eternal life; and these are they which bear witness of me; and ye will not come to me, that ye may have life." The "me" here refers not to Jesus, but to the "I AM" Self within. Could it be more clear that you may be trying to find salvation from the Bible, when it can only be found within yourself?

The Bible and its eternal message deal, not alone with God or with Jesus, but with you and the discovery and unleashing of the power of your innate divinity. This great Truth is yet to be discovered, across the board, in all the divisions and schisms of Christianity. It has been the best kept secret of the ages. Paul certainly had caught this vision, for he referred to "the mystery hidden for ages and generations . . . which is Christ in you, the hope of glory" (Col. 1:26–27 RSV).

With all the getting of education and academic degrees, there is a need to become wise in transcendent ways. In our study of the Bible we must realize that its Truth does not come *to* you, but *through* you. Its wisdom is not in the written words, but in the Word of Truth that they reveal. And the central figure of the Scripture is not Jesus, but the Christ, the transcendent Self that Jesus discovered within himself, which he revealed as being within ourselves. And the whole purpose of it all is the discovery and unleashing from within ourselves of the power to become what we innately are and of the personal revelation of the wisdom of the ages.

Great wisdom is certainly to be found in the Bible, but it is not necessarily found in reading the literal text. Modern Bible scholarship has revealed many startling facts that have shed light on many of the confusing doctrines of Christianity. Many idioms and metaphors should be seen only in the light of contemporary usage. For instance, when Jesus said the fisherman-disciple should go out on the lake, where he would find a gold coin in a fish's mouth, he was referring metaphorically to the fact that the disciples, as fishermen, should bring in a catch of fish which could be sold at the market to realize the wherewithal to pay their taxes. The metaphor of "gold in the fish's mouth" is on a par with the Oriental metaphor of "the oxen have thirty pieces of silver in their horns." Or the Western cattle rancher's boast that the prime steer is worth "forty dollars on the hoof."

Also, the Bible is steeped in symbolism and can only be understood in a metaphysical or personally symbolic sense. For instance, the book of Job is a play, with a vital spiritual message for every person on the path of enlightenment. Job was a fictitious character, symbolically blazing a trail from self-righteousness to spiritual consciousness. Job reveals the step that will enable us to make the transition from suffering to wholeness of mind, body, and affairs. The many wisdom messages of the Bible can lead us to self-knowledge and self-realization if we insist on moving from the symbolic to the real.

A continually expanding metaphysical treatment of Scripture can be an excellent guide for life in the coming years of the third millennium. We must know that the supreme power of the Universe is not locked in ancient scriptures—whether the Judeo-Christian or the holy works of the religions of the East; they are alive in the world today. Revelation is not a special dispensation of God, but a quality of Divine Mind and a faculty of the mind of every person. Further, what God is revealing to people today may be more important than what He said to certain ones yesterday.

This is a point where our churches have failed us. Conservative religion is religion in retrospect. The key emphasis is always on the prophets of antiquity, the great historic creeds, the rites, rituals, and traditions of other days. Emerson, one of the most notorious uncommonsense thinkers, said, "Why cannot we have first-hand and immediate experience of God?" Why must we worship in retrospect? Why not a presence of God that is present here and now? Why not a religion that is practical and not just historical and orthodox?

PRACTICAL CHRISTIANITY

We frequently hear a Truth student waxing ecstatic about Truth, "Why, practical Christianity is just common sense!" This is a dangerous trap, for it isn't common sense at all. Such a characterization may lead us to attempt to bring the dynamic Truths into the tone of the common point of view. Jesus taught that all things are possible to them that believe. Common sense will say, "Of course, he didn't mean *all* things." Ah, but he did! There is much confusion about the "silent years" in the New Testament story about Jesus, when it leaves him as a boy of twelve and does not return to him again until he is a full-grown man entering his ministry. It gives the key to the conscious evolution of his greatness in a single sentence: "Jesus increased in wisdom and in stature, and in favor with God and man" (Lk. 2:52 RSV). Before we shy away from the word "perfection," let us consider what St. Augustine had to say about it. "If thou shouldst say, 'It is enough, I have reached perfection'—all is lost. For it is the function of perfection to make one know one's imperfections."

It is a key to understanding the Garden of Eden story—what is called "The Fall of Man." The philosopher calls it "the fall upward." It is symbolic of the process of evolution. So Adam and Eve were driven from the garden, not by God's vindictiveness, but by the functioning of divine law. As Adam and Eve awakened in consciousness, they knew how unevolved they were. So they consciously moved out of the Garden to evolve and work for "worthship."

In the Garden of Eden, in a personally symbolic sense, we emerged into consciousness and discovered the law of mind-action, which says that where you are in experience is a certain and quite dependable reflection of where you happen to be in consciousness.

Wherever you are right now, no matter what you may be experiencing, you are in your right place. It may not be where you want to be at all. And it is not where you need to be. Where you are is the situation that corresponds to your mentality at the moment. But you can change. It can be, and should be, a place of growth. It is the best possible place in which to do the growing you need to do to realize the outformation of your God Self.

This was the discovery of Job. He wondered why he was where he was, but in time he realized it was his right place—the place where he could work out the limited states of his consciousness, so that he could get into the experience which was his true place. Thus, the very first step in conscious evolution is the discovery of the role of mind and the need to move toward mental management.

XII
77
XXI

ROLE OF THE MIND

In its more primitive use, mind is simply a reflex of experience. Things happen and we react, and thus we become worried, fearful, angry. We assume that our thought is produced by circumstances and that our upsets, our fears, our worries are caused by the conditions we are upset or fearful or worried about. This is not really true, and it is a great discovery just to realize it. We worry and are fearful simply because that is the way, by habit or by choice, we meet the situation. We can always meet it in a different way—in love or peace or nonresistance. We can always determine, and we should, that we will not permit things or persons to decide how we are going to think or act.

Thus, a commonsense form of religion, call it "Liberal Christianity," modifies the old concepts to fit into the mold of human consciousness, making them common sense. But there is a great difference between Liberal Christianity and Practical Christianity. The former makes the message more acceptable by watering down the ideas to conform with the consensus of the known. The latter renders the ideas in a form that can be understood, enabling us to put them to work in everyday experience. The one circumvents the fundamentals to make them easier to live *with*; the other catches the spirit of the teaching to make it easier to live *by*.

Harvard University professor/poet/philosopher George Santayana addresses an urgent problem of mankind:

> O world, thou choosest not the better part!
> It is not wisdom to be only wise,
> And on the inward vision close the eyes,
> But it is wisdom to believe the heart.
> Columbus found a world, and had no chart,
> Save one that faith deciphered in the skies;
> To trust the soul's invincible surmise

Was all his science and his only art.
Our knowledge is a torch of smoky pine
That lights the pathway but one step ahead
Across a void of mystery and dread.
Bid, then, the tender light of faith to shine
By which alone the mortal heart is led
Unto the thinking of the thought divine.

We subject ourselves to a lot of flattery about the marvels of science and technology that have come forth from the intellect of man. We make rash comments, such as, "If we can put a man on the moon, we certainly should be able to find the answers to war, poverty, pollution, and AIDS."

The interesting thing, perhaps the frightening thing, is that the more we apply our intellect toward solutions to our problems, even feeding all aspects of the problems into our mind-created computers, the more confused we seem to become. The answer, as in the case of the prodigal son, is to "come to ourselves." We need to wake up to who we are: spiritual beings, channels for the expression of infinite wisdom through our intellect. We are transcendent creatures, and we can never rise to the greatness of our divine potential unless we cultivate our own transcendence—through inner listening, meditation, and prayer.

WISDOM OF THE HEART

An article in *Time* magazine quotes Einstein as saying that all his work was the result of intuition, an inner feeling, and not from logic and reason. Of course, he ultimately had to use the intellect to devise the "proof" that would satisfy the scientific community and to devise practical methods with which to put the revelation to use.

Thinking of Einstein confirms the wisdom of Santayana: "It is not wisdom to be only wise, and on the inward vision close the eyes. But it is wisdom to believe the heart." So Einstein was not just a great intellect. He was, first of all, a great lover, whose great wisdom came from believing the heart.

Emerson says, "There is one mind common to all individual persons . . . and by lowly listening we shall hear the right word." Christian tradition has erred in insisting that the "right word" is the literal application of the Bible, or a series of cliches, such as, "You must be born again." But the "right word" is the word of Truth, the spiritual counterpart of that which concerns you. When you have a challenge, your prayer is going into the secret place within and lowly listening. And the "right word" felt is the affirmative realization.

Then the prayer process entails affirming this word of Truth, not to make it true, but to get yourself centered in the cosmic flow. It could be said that there is an affirmation to correspond spiritually with every human need. However, the power is not in the affirmation, but in the Truth that it articulates. Jesus gives an important perspective when he says, "The word which you hear is not mine but the Father's who sent me" (Jn. 14:24 RSV). Through "lowly listening" we hear the right word, the word of Truth. It is God pronouncing His works as very good. When I lowly listen, I do not *affirm* the Truth of being but, rather, I *confirm* the Truth of *Being, being me.*

WISDOM IN EDUCATION

Obviously, there is a need for training in the art of "lowly listening." This has been a "no-no" in education, because it sounds like "religion." But this is a hang-up we must outgrow in our society. Certainly, separation of church and state is a good thing, because it prevents the possibility of a state religion that could become a political tool. But we cannot go on perpetuating the delusion that everything transcendent to the five-sense person is religious and therefore off-limits to educators and the educational process.

H. G. Wells, so prophetic in so many fields, in his novel *Men Like Gods* visioned a time when schools and teachers would no longer be necessary, except to show us how to get in touch with the infinite knowledge that indwells us in the Mind of Minds. Startling as this seems, it might well be the subject of serious discussion among educators in the third millennium.

Bonnie Day, from the book *Best Loved Unity Poems*, creates a character that could have been the product of such a school. Listen:

> The depths of metaphysical law
>   She little grasped or understood;
> Yet with clear eyes of faith she saw
>   One shining Truth . . . that God is good.
> She could not quote one single line
>   Of affirmation, tenet, creed;
> But how she trusted Love Divine
>   To meet her every human need.
>
> Hers was a plain theology
>   That love could swiftly comprehend;
> Her whole religion was to be
>   To all who needed her . . . a friend.
> The laws of science and of art
>   She made no claim to understand;
> But love was law within her heart,
>   And kindness . . . law unto her hand.
>
> A wisdom never learned from books
>   But tutored by an inward grace
> Was written in her very looks

And shone reflected in her face.
In thought profound, and creed sublime,
She builded better than she knew . . .
A doctrine that shall outlast time:
To trust . . . to love . . . to be . . . and do.

It's not Shakespeare . . . but it is a classic about a wisdom that is more than wise. It gives a helpful perspective on the philosophy of education.

THE DAWN OF TRANSCENDENCE

The great need of our day is the belief in the depth of the person, the transcendence of life, the universality of Mind, and the wisdom to believe the heart. The great frustration of the potentiality of people today may be directly traceable to the virtual absence of meditation in their way of life. I am referring not to a ritual of postures and positions and chants, but to a new sense of the flow of life and the need to keep conscious that life is lived from within-out, to know that creative ideas do not come *to* us, but *through* us and that we are cocreators with God. When we face insurmountable problems, such as we do today, the way out is in.

We admire people who have expressed great intelligence or creativity. But we do not realize that we live and move and have being in the same Mind-force. Didn't Paul say, "Let this mind be in you, which was also in Christ Jesus"? (Phil. 2:5 KJV) Thus to *find* God, to *understand* God, we need to expand our thoughts to the realization of the omnipresence of God and know that the whole of Spirit is present in its entirety, at every point in space at the same time. There is no distance between you and God. There is nowhere to go for wisdom and intuitive leadings. We are in the field of infinite Intelligence, all the time. Thus God is present always and in all ways.

God knows. God knows . . . in you. Knowing *is* . . . and it is at hand. It is *now*. The way out of all conflict is at hand.

This calls for a new concept of God. Emerson speaks to the millennial theology that is evolving, as he says, "When we have broken with our god of tradition, and ceased from our god of rhetoric, then may God fire the heart with His presence." God is not a wise Superperson in a lofty realm "out there." He is Wisdom itself. He is the Allness in which you exist as an "eachness." Wherever you may be, the whole of infinite Mind is present in its entirety, and you live and have being in this Mind. The implications of this are awesome. It dramatically changes our perception of God and of prayer. It changes forever our image of God as a person to whom we pray, into a cosmic flow of life, substance, and intelligence by which we live. Thus, we do not pray *to* God for or about anything. Rather we pray *from* the consciousness of God. "Be still, and know that I am God" (Ps. 46:10 RSV). Prayer is not an attempt to get God to come to our rescue; rather, it is a refocusing of our consciousness from the appearance of lack and limitation to the reality of wholeness.

Eventually, we will begin to experience ourselves as a point of consciousness in the boundless Universe—and as a channel for the expression of the energy of love, of the wisdom of the heart and of the faith to go forth centered in living light. Meditate regularly for fifteen minutes once a day, at least, and you will soon find yourself emerging from the experience relaxed and refreshed, as well as being able to function as a whole person and seeing things in the context of the wholeness of life. You will behave more *spontaneously*, and what you say and do will be *sincere* and *simple* and *sane*.

In our effort to heal the problems of the world, we will have to have the daring and wisdom to believe the heart—to begin to let the answers unfold, through inner guidance and intuitive knowing and in love and faith.

As we enter the new millennium, humankind is on the verge of a great breakthrough—a spiritual renaissance. The day of intellectualism is over, and the dawn of transcendence, of intuition, of the wisdom that comes from the heart is upon us.

Eric Butterworth, ordained in 1948, has been a leading minister in Unity and New Thought for fifty years. A past president of the Association of Unity Churches, he speaks every Sunday at Avery Fisher Hall at New York's Lincoln Center at a nondenominational service he calls "An Experience of Creative Worthship."

Eric is a pioneer radio broadcaster. His program *Eric Butterworth Speaks* has been on the air seven days a week for over forty years. He's been featured on CBS across the country and by shortwave around the world.

Eric Butterworth has written fourteen books, including the best-selling *Discover the Power Within You* and *Spiritual Economics*, both considered to be classics in the New Thought field. Eric's books have been translated into five languages.

CHAPTER V

THE POWER OF IMAGINATION

The power of imagination is linked closely with the power of faith, for the perceiving power and the conceiving power are closely related. Perceiving has more to do with awareness, however, and is a little more passive; conceiving, like when we conceive a child, is a little more proactive! Imagination, then, is a conceiving power, a faculty of mind that images, shapes, and forms thoughts.

It is a truism in New Thought that what we conceive and believe, we become. James Dillet Freeman, whose imagination has helped thousands of minds to soar along with him, knows this better than most. As one of New Thought's most disciplined and talented writers, he knows how much imagination by itself is sterile. It leads to vain imaginings. More than most of the powers, imagination needs the other powers to stimulate, support, and ground its efforts. Without imagination, however, we would be hard pressed to create anything new or break out of the bonds of yesterday's thinking.

Bartholomew, son of Tolmai, called Nathanael in the first chapter of John, represents the power of imagination. According to Charles Fillmore, Jesus discerned his presence under the fig tree before he came into visibility. Imagination, then, in order to serve the higher cause of spirituality, requires the power of discernment and wisdom, just to be brought forth.

Imagination: The Wondrous Power of Conception

James Dillet Freeman

My imagination and I have had an off-and-on love affair that began before I can remember. We love one another and sometimes we can't draw apart, but sometimes we can't get together. Sometimes I come running after her, demanding that she tell me what's going on; sometimes she comes running after me, demanding that I listen to what I would rather not hear.

I learned long ago that I can't tell her what to say; I have to ask *her* what she wants to say. Then I have to listen very closely and quickly put down what she tells me. Sometimes to my wonder and surprise, there spring forth, like sparks from a divine fire,

> Visions of faith, insights of love,
> Truths that I had no forethought of.

Imagination has been a rich and wondrous world for me. What a joy it is to have your imagination suddenly reveal to you a truth that was not there before or a beauty you did not see until it revealed itself to you. Sometimes when I stop writing, I feel that I am floating eight feet above the floor and can't get back down.

86

Imagination is "the act or power of forming a mental image of something not present to the senses or never before wholly perceived in reality." Here, then, is a power that frees us from the limitations of our senses. When we imagine something, we have a revelation and a vision not through our senses, but by the creative action of our mind. Imagination is the power of conception.

> I fly, but not on wings,
> I soar, but not through sky;
> Where no bird ever flings
> Itself in flight, fly I!
> For birds are bound by air
> As to their course of flight,
> But thought's my thoroughfare,
> And who can take its height?

THE POWER TO IMAGINE

We have often heard that we human beings have evolved to be what we are because we have the power to reason, and this is true. Ability to reason has been no small part of the reason we have grown to be what we are. But no less important has been our power to imagine. It has given us the power to see that we may be more than we seem to be and that our world may have possibilities for growth and change beyond any which it has disclosed. Reason may direct our courses, but it is imagination that tells us yet more is to be found in us and in our world and entices us to see if we can bring forth what the "yet more" may be. The imagination of Daedalus conceived and created the inescapable labyrinth in Crete in which he was imprisoned, but his imagination also conceived the waxen wings on which he and his son Icarus rose from its depths—he to creative life, because his imagination was tempered by reason and good judgment, and Icarus to death, because his pride blinded him to the fact that his wings were of wax and would melt when the light of the sun shone fully upon them.

Imagination may become a blessing or a curse, depending on how well we have developed some of the other powers of our mind and spirit. We are born with this faculty already highly developed in us, and it is a chief enrichment in our life. It is our imagination that gives us hope of being more than we seem to be. Imagination is the creative faculty of the mind, and many of the most useful, productive, and extraordinary works in the world of us human beings begin as works of the imagination.

Think about this and you will see how true it is. I sit at a desk, which is the work of imagination; I write with a pencil, which is the work of imagination; I write by an electric light, which is the work of imagination; I wear eyeglasses and a watch, which are works of imagination; I wear clothes of 35% polyester, which are all works of imagination; etc. & etc.—and the "ampersand" and the "etcetera" are also works of imagination.

Our imagination has profound effects on our mental state and whether we are happy or unhappy persons may depend as much on what we habitually imagine our world to be as on what our world actually is. However, only when imagination is joined with the will, with good judgment as to the worth of its works, and with the power to do the work—often tedious—to give the images it produces in the mind a physical form in the outer world can it change the outer world. Still, many of the realest things in our world of things began as visions of the mind.

THE LAW OF MIND ACTION

One of the great teachings of Unity is the law of mind action: "Thoughts held in mind produce in the outer after their kind." Charles Fillmore taught over and over that it is the law of mind action which shapes our world. Our world is what our mental processes—our senses and perceptions, feelings and emotions, logical thoughts, passionate desires, and imagination—decree it to be.

Why are there so much misery and pain in our world? I don't know about you. I hope you are more of a positive thinker than I am. I find myself continually thinking thoughts and feeling feelings of fear, worry, anger, guilt, confusion, and various other negative varieties. I am constantly trying to turn off such thoughts and turn on more positive ones. When I turn my thoughts free to go where they will, I often find myself having something negative happening in my imagination. That the imagination of most of us is more likely to be negative than positive is shown by how many more words there are in our dictionaries to describe unhappy states than happy ones. Dante's *Inferno* is much more vivid than his *Paradiso*.

Imagination is the most entertaining and most frightening of all our faculties. It is the conjurer. It can beguile and bewitch us; it can frighten or enlighten us; it can lift us to ecstasy or plunge us to despair.

If we let it run unrestrained, it may take over our life. Many of us live in our imagination almost as much as in our outer world. When we have things to meet, instead of meeting them with faithful prayer and firm action, we meet them in our imagination, but what occurs in our imagination may not be at all what is actually occurring. Our imagination may just be playacting what our hopes *hope* is happening or what our fears *fear* is happening.

Our mind is busy every moment. When it is not under our conscious direction, it is just as active as when we are telling it what to think. If we have formed the habit of letting our mind dream up unhappy circumstances and events, it will do so whether we want it to or not.

In the early days of Unity, denial was almost as important a part of Unity's methods of prayer as affirmation. Every moment, a thought is entering our mind and we are saying *yes* or *no* to it.

XII

89

XXI

That is why Paul tells us we should try to "pray without ceasing" (1 Thess. 5:17 KJV). Unless we keep our minds consciously turned toward God, we are likely to find that we have formed the habit of drifting unconsciously into troubled and troubling imaginings.

Among the powers of the mind, imagination is the magician. We have always believed in magic.

We human beings learned long ago that we had a power in us which can call forth the likeness of things and that if we concentrate it on gaining some single aim and hold to it with all our will, it may call forth the thing itself. This is the magic of prayer, if not the prayer of magic. Human beings have always used this kind of prayer.

IMAGINATION AND THE OTHER POWERS

Imagination must be combined with other faculties of mind and heart to bring forth the blessings it is capable of achieving. Ideas are just ideas, nothing more, whatever their origin—be it imagination, observation, intuition, reason, or revelation—until we do something with them. Until we have the energy to take the idea, the mental image, and give it form in the world of things, it is a mere wisp of thought, without substance or power. When we combine it with some of our other God-given powers, then it may change not only us, but all the world.

One of the most imaginative men of this or any other time was Thomas Alva Edison. He showed us by his life and works what great achievements imagination can produce and what it needs to produce them. He said, "Genius is one percent inspiration and ninety-nine percent perspiration."

Life asks more of us than just visualizing some desire and demanding its fulfillment, as if we were a spoiled child. We are children, but we are children of God. We need to develop qualities of heart and mind, like courage and love and strength and calmness and intelligence. When we have these, we have fulfillment.

I have, however, had a number of unusual things happen in my life, making me feel that, although I need to develop more powers than my imagination, I should not underestimate the power which comes from keeping a clear vision of what I want and holding to it and pouring my will and energy into bringing it about.

For instance, when the time came for me to go to college, the world was at the bottom of the Great Depression and I had been told that there would be no money for an education. However, it had never occurred to me that I was not going to be a college-educated man, so with only $64 pinned in my vest pocket and no assurance of another penny, I quit my job, got on a bus, and headed for school. I don't believe I have ever felt lower than that evening when I got off the bus, not knowing a soul in town, not having any idea where I would live or how I would make my living, not even knowing where the university was located. But that very evening a series of strange and unpredictable events occurred which made it possible not only for me to stay in school until I graduated, but to graduate with honors, to become student-body president, to win literary contests, and even to have a year's postgraduate work—and with all this, to have a comfortable room with a private bath!

Forty years ago my wife and I lived in a small house and ardently wanted to live in a more beautiful one. We spent many hours looking at new houses, but the ones we longed for cost more than we had. To get to Lee's Summit, Missouri, from Unity Village, we often drove on a back road. We didn't even know the name of the road, but behind a white rail fence on this road was a beautiful farmhouse. Behind this was a beautiful tenant house. Behind this was a beautiful white barn. It was all so beautiful that every time we drove by it, we would say, "We hope those people are taking good care of our house." We had no idea that we could afford to live in such a place, but one day a friend who was a real estate agent was visiting us. He said: "Jim, why don't you move to Lee's Summit; it would be closer to your work."

I said: "Oh, I don't see any reason to live in Lee's Summit. I am close enough now." But then I added: "Yes, there is a house." And I described it to him.

He said, "That's interesting. They want to sell that farm and I am the agent."

They wanted far more money than we could pay for the farm, but a few months later they told us they would sell us just enough land, about two acres, to include the big house, the little house, and half the barn, and they loaned us the money to buy it. They had to include half the barn because the barn was only three feet behind the little house. I wonder if anyone else, to buy a house, has bought half a barn.

I have lived in our house for forty years.

I have had enough such events happen that I have come to believe that if there is not a prayer of magic, there is certainly a magic in prayer, and imagination is no small part of it. Jesus said, "Ask, and it will be given you" (Mt. 7:7). I believe this, but I think you will agree that this needs considerable metaphysical interpretation. Unity says there is a law of mind action and I believe this, but I think this needs explanation too.

Powerful as imagination is, it is not powerful enough that by itself it can change our world. It has almost limitless power over our thought world, but over the world of things, it has power only when it is combined with other powers. The world is not what it is because we imagine it to be that. The world we live in is not an imaginary one. We don't change it by creating a mental image of some other world we would rather be in. Nowhere did Jesus say, "According to your imagination, be it done." He said, "According to your faith be it done to you" (Mt. 9:29 RSV). The world is what our faith tells us it is. Faith is not imagining. Faith is not making believe that something *is* that isn't. It is believing and making something *be* that isn't. Imagination may turn on a light, but faith turns on the power. When we think of imagination, we think of wings. When we think of faith, we think of a rock. Wings can carry us to new adventures, but it is upon the rock of faith that we build a life.

Is there a limit to our power of imagination? Thousands of religions have set up thousands of images to show us what God is like. In the twentieth chapter of Exodus, God says, "You shall not make for yourself a graven image, or any likeness of anything that is in heaven above, or that is in the earth beneath, or that is in the water under the earth; you shall not bow down to them or serve them; for I the Lord your God am a jealous God" (Ex. 20:4–5 RSV). We can't imagine God; God imagined us—that is how we came into being. All we can truly say is that God is God.

DREAMS AND DAYDREAMS

If we want to see clearly what imagination is and what are its powers and its limits, let us look at our dreams. Here imagination rules supreme. Do you have any idea how much of our life we spend in dreams? Most of us sleep about eight hours every night, and psychologists tell us that we are dreaming in at least four of them. The ancients taught there is both dreaming and dreamless slumber. Whether or not, we have at least four hours of dreams every night and we have almost no idea of what happens in them.

We wake from dreams and we remember that in the dream we were living in a world which is not at all the world our senses present to us. A dream world is full of persons and conditions utterly unlike the world where we carry on our life when we are awake. Many ancient people considered their dream world to be as real as their daytime world or perhaps even *more* real. The messages brought back from it were believed to have special meaning and power.

And the dreams we have when we are sleeping are only part of our dream life. When we are not consciously directing our thinking, as in solving problems or in prayers, we are likely to be imagining something that we are daydreaming. Many persons deny that they daydream, but the fact is that most of us live in our imagination a great deal of the time.

Perhaps *daydream* seems a very unreal name for this very real part of our life. *Fantasy,* another term, does not give a much more substantial feeling. By *daydream* I mean the playacting life we live in our imagination. Life brings us something to meet, and we meet it not by doing things or saying things in the outer world, but by imagining doing and saying things in the inner.

Long before we learned to think with words, dreams and fantasies were the forms our thoughts took. When we have something to meet that involves our emotions, we are still likely to think about it in terms of fantasy and dream. We bring the people and conditions involved onto the stage of our mind, and we act out our response to them in a play that our hopes and desires, our fears and angers write as we perform it.

To most of us, I believe the outer life is more real and vivid than the inner one. But sometimes the life we live in our daydreams is more exciting than the one we live in the flesh-and-blood physical world. To some, and for most of us at certain times, this inner life is the one that is most meaningful.

Our daydreams may sometimes be negative and may become a way of avoiding, rather than meeting, our problems. But also they may be positive. Probably most of the world's songs and symphonies, poems, plays, stories, inventions, scientific discoveries, religions, business enterprises, and political movements have begun in dreams and daydreams. Without them how much less our life would be! Sometimes our dreams and daydreams expand and flower and find creative forms that not only enrich the dreamer's life, but also the life of the whole human race.

Dreams and imagination had a great role in the founding of Unity. Charles and Myrtle Fillmore both wrote articles about dreams and their interpretation.

XII

94

XXI

"It [imagination]," Mr. Fillmore wrote, "is the maker in us of forms and shapes. In contour, your body is the result of your imagination. So every time you look into the glass, you can see yourself as you appear or seem to be in your mind.

"Cultivate imagination; be true to the heavenly vision. Picture in your mind continually that which you want to be and refuse to judge according to appearances."

Mr. Fillmore said that although he saw his wife get healing through prayer, in the beginning of his search for God he found the statements of Truth teachers so muddled and conflicting that he said to himself: "In this babel I will go to headquarters. If I am Spirit and this God they talk so much about is Spirit, we can somehow communicate, or the whole thing is a fraud." He commenced sitting in the silence every night at a certain hour and tried to get in touch with God. He kept at this month after month, mentally affirming words and leaving his mind open to receive inspiration, and the time came when he realized that in his dreams he was finding communication with God as the source of Truth and guidance in his life, and Unity began.

XII

95

XXI

JESUS AND PARABLES

Jesus knew the compelling power of imagination. Jesus was a poet. When they asked him what heaven is, he answered that it is like a mustard seed or a little leaven or a treasure hidden in a field. That is a poet's answer. When he wanted to show God's relationship to us, he called God our "Father." That is a poet's epithet. There is no greater poem in literature than his Sermon on the Mount.

When Jesus had a message that he felt was especially important for people to understand, he often delivered his message in the form of a parable. In fact, The Gospels tell us that Jesus "said nothing to them without a parable" (Mt. 13:34 RSV). Disciples asked him, "Why do you speak to them in parables?" Jesus said, "This is why I speak to them in parables, because seeing they do not see, and hearing they do not hear, nor do they understand" (Mt. 13:10, 13 RSV). Parables are the language of the imagination.

A CHILDLIKE IMAGINATION

If you want to see what a powerful influence imagination has on our life, look at children. Children are the embodiment of imagination; they continually retreat into its world. Perhaps it is truer to say that they live in it and only occasionally emerge into our real one.

Matthew, Mark, and Luke all tell how Jesus took children in his arms and said that only those who had a mind and spirit like children would enter the kingdom of God. Jesus "said to them, 'Let the children come to me, do not hinder them; for to such belongs the kingdom of God. Truly, I say to you, whoever does not receive the kingdom of God like a child shall not enter it" (Mk. 10:14–15 RSV).

Maybe we upright, mature, so-sure-we-know-the-way men and women should look and see what a child is like.

When we were children I think we knew we were all members of the same universal human family of God. It takes time for us to learn the grown-up language of "dos and don'ts," "rights and wrongs," "hates and fears." We are the children of Life and Love in a world that Life and Love has made, and until grown-ups teach us this is not the way it is, we try to live as if it were. If we grown-ups had the courage to believe that Love made us and the world, I wonder if that is not the way we and the world would turn out to be. And do we not at least occasionally imagine such a world?

We grown-up people, hardened with habit and encased in fact, go from commonplace to commonplace. To children there are no ordinary things or ordinary people. The most ordinary things are just as wonderful and strange as extraordinary things are. When we are children, we know that things are only partly fact. They are mostly imagination. Facts are just miracles that we have found an explanation for. You and I and everything else in the world have an infinite potential. We have not yet learned that there are impossibles.

> Do not ask a child to tell
> You what is a miracle;
> He may turn and ask you what
> In all the world you think is not.

Children have faith that they are God's children in God's world. They have to learn after they get here that this world is not divine, but mundane. How do they learn this? We grown-ups teach them. We muddy down their faith that this is a good world made by a good God with our race belief that we are limited beings living in a world of limited resources. Einstein's formula $E = mc^2$ shows how right the children are. How did Einstein arrive at his unbelievable truth? He said that he asked the questions a child would ask.

The central teaching of Unity is this: There is only one Presence and one Power in the universe—God, the Good and Omnipotent. I don't think children know any such words, but I think they know how true this is. I think that children know what they are meant to be, for I think there has never been a child who did not feel the stirring of divinity within. They know that they have all they can possibly need to become all they can possibly be and that all they have to do is be what God made them to be.

Every child is the product of perfection's hungering to bring forth a perfect thing, and all the forces of heaven and earth converge around the birth to help the child to be more than anything she or he has ever been before.

THE HUNGER FOR PERFECTION

Imagination is one of the ways this hunger for perfection expresses itself. We imagine a better us, a better life, a better world, and we seek to bring it into manifestation. Today we live in an age of imagination. It began about five hundred years ago when men began to break down the walls that the church had erected to ensure the unquestioning acceptance of its doctrines, forbidding people to think for themselves. But here and there intelligent people looked at the church and the world and began to observe and question and wonder.

The Bible and other writings were translated out of the Latin that only priests learned into the language the people spoke. Gutenberg invented the printing press—a great work of the imagination—so instead of a few priestly manuscripts, hundreds of books and leaflets were soon scattered around Europe, and thinking men and women could share one another's thoughts.

When a little Polish monk named Copernicus published his book, asserting that the earth did not stand still but circled around the sun, he wisely arranged for the publication to be delayed until after his death. Soon men like Galileo and Kepler and scores of other astronomers were discovering all sorts of fascinating new truths about the heavens. They are still discovering them. Once Luther had nailed his ninety-five theses on the door of the castle church in Wittenberg and started the Protestant Reformation, scores of new interpretations of Christianity appeared and are continuing to appear. Unity is one of them.

Imagination feeds on its own inventiveness. Discovery leads to yet further discoveries. Every new truth we find throws light on yet newer truths to be found.

Roentgen discovered the X ray in 1895, and Pierre and Marie Curie isolated radium in 1898; the physical world that had seemed so unshakably solid began to fall apart. From this new subatomic world of particles, waves, energy, and emptiness, physicists are extracting ever more marvelous secrets and powers.

This last century especially has seen a stream of discoveries that have changed every area of our life. We even see new ideas in religion. The old established religions are changing the way they carry out their worship services and are relinquishing their narrow claim to exclusive knowledge of the truth. We see the advent of dozens of New Thought religions promoting Hindu and Buddhist ideas like Yoga and Zen, but in a Western version that is not an abandonment of the scientific advances which have given us such control of the world of things. They show us how to meet our practical needs, as well as how to unfold our spiritual nature.

To flourish, imagination must be encouraged to flourish. No, that is not a strong enough statement. Imagination must be left free to roam! It may venture into wildernesses—and it must, if it is to chart new roads. We may bemoan the ludicrous, immoral, and dangerous ideas and practices it sometimes may proclaim, and we may call its promoters heretics and hippies, rebels and radicals, atheists and anarchists—and such they may be! But we must not let our fixed habits of thought and behavior so overwhelm our tolerance that we keep growth from occurring. The church did that, and for more than a thousand years, the Western world stood still.

Two thousand years ago when a council wanted to kill some people who were presenting the radical new idea that Jesus was Savior, a man named Gamaliel told them: "Keep away from these men and let them alone; for if this plan or this undertaking is of men, it will fail; but if it is of God, you will not be able to overthrow them. You might even be found opposing God!" (Acts 5:38–39 RSV)

TOWARD A NEW MILLENNIUM

Most of us today, looking back at the wars and the violence and the misery that have plagued the last thousand years, are wondering if there is not a better way for us to live together than we have fashioned in the past.

We have created so many wonders that have changed our way of life in so many areas, can we not devise ways for nations as well as individuals to live together in peace?

XII

99

XXI

A couple of events have occurred that give us hope:

1. A terrible war ended fifty years ago and the victors, instead of pillaging and ravaging the losers, who had started this war, helped them to find prosperity and stability, so much so that today the losers are among the most prosperous and progressive of nations.

2. You may criticize President Truman for dropping the nuclear bomb that ended this war. Consider, however, how the United States then had in its hands a weapon no nation could stand against, but instead of using it to take control of the earth, the United States promoted the United Nations and took its place in this new league—not as the ruling nation, but as one nation alongside other nations. Some who read this may not think the United Nations is an effective organization, but it has lasted almost half a century now and it has grown. Who can doubt it is a step forward? At least, human beings are trying to join in a common effort, whatever their differences of race or religion, to solve problems; to share resources, skills, and powers; to help one another to a better way of life in a world of peace.

Imagination will not let us or the world stand still.

Five hundred years ago our world was a few hundred thousand square miles of land, mostly unexplored, hardly any of it mapped, lying flat under a mysterious heaven surrounded by unknown seas. It had edges that you might fall off if you went too far. Two hundred years ago we could travel no faster than a horse could carry us; a yoke of oxen or a water wheel was the limit of our power. One hundred years ago we were still setting out to sea in wooden ships with sails.

Today we make our journeys in ships that fly through the air. We explore the stars. We dream of building cities in space. Twelve men have walked on the moon. They flew there in space ships at thousands of miles an hour, and when the first man climbed down the ladder from his rocket ship onto the moon, we were there with him. We saw his boots kick up moondust. We heard him exclaim, "That's one small step for [a] man, one giant leap for mankind."

We watch and talk with people on the other side of the earth. We give the sick a new heart and bring them back from death. We have doubled our lifespan. We warm the winter and cool the summer. We have split the infinitesimal atom and laid hold of its incalculable powers.

Every single one of our achievements, every single blessing we enjoy, we enjoy only because someone who had come to the farthest edge of knowledge and been told that was as far as anyone could go said, "Perhaps, but I wonder." Someone refused to settle for what *seems* to be. Someone dared to ask his or her mind, "Have you yet more to reveal?" And in the mind a light shown and cast a glow, and in that glow there was yet more to be found.

And the age of the creative imagination is only beginning. Do not believe that we will conquer the brute forces of nature and not the brute forces in our own nature. Do not believe that we will find the center of the atom and not our own center. Do not believe that we will master the world outside ourselves and not the world inside ourselves.

Has our exploration of the outer world opened windows on infinity? The world within us is no less an infinity. The Master told us, "Seek, and you will find" (Mt. 7:7 RSV). He placed no limits on our growth. He said, "Whatsoever ye shall ask in prayer, believing, ye shall receive" (Mt. 21:22 KJV).

A few years ago I wrote a book entitled *The Hilltop Heart.* At its end I stood on the hilltop that is my heart and I had this vision of the world we are on the way to bringing forth:

> If we just keep at the task—the human world divine that this man-god, god-man in us can grasp and shape if he but will!
>
> A world where the battle is not of men against men, but of man against the darkness.
>
> A world where brutality becomes brotherhood.
>
> A living world, a happy world, a world of works undreamed of, a world that is a fitting habitation for the human heart and mind.

A world where nations cooperate with one another—and compete with one another, not out of the craving for conquest, but like runners in a race who compete out of the desire to excel.

A world where all people have a chance to develop the potential they were born with.

A world where you and I are free to live as we will, but where we will to live for one another.

The world of which the Master dreamed when He said, "Ye are gods . . . children of the most High . . ."

What we conceive today, what we imagine with hearts and minds full of faith and love and strength, the next millennium will be. We will have made it so. We get what we really, really believe.

Called the "Poet Laureate to the Moon" or "a modern-day Ralph Waldo Emerson," **James Dillet Freeman** has been the most popular of all Unity writers. His poetry has been read by more than five hundred million people.

Jim Freeman has had his work taken to the moon twice, a distinction he shares with no other author. His 1941 "Prayer for Protection" was taken aboard Apollo 11 in July 1969 by Lunar Module pilot Edwin E. Aldrin, Jr. Aldrin had the poem with him when he made his historic moonwalk! Two years later, Jim's 1947 poem "I Am There" went to the moon with Colonel James B. Irwin on Apollo 15. Irwin left a microfilm copy of the poem on the moon.

Jim has published twelve books, some by Doubleday, Harper & Row and some by Unity Books, including *The Hilltop Heart, The Case for Reincarnation,* and *Once Upon a Christmas.* His books have been translated into thirteen languages. He has been published in *The New Yorker, Saturday Review, Scientific Monthly, The New York Times, Christian Herald, Reader's Digest,* and many others.

CHAPTER VI

THE POWER OF ZEAL

Zeal is the power of intensity and enthusiasm. It, like imagination, is what fires our souls and helps us over the hurdles of life, including the part of our being that wants to keep us safe and secure and tied to the way things were.

Zeal, too, needs the help of the other powers, particularly the power of wisdom, for zeal can run rampant, consuming our life force, our energy, in its singleminded pursuit of its goals. A little zeal is absolutely necessary; a lot of zeal needs to be tempered by wisdom, the power that involves judgment and spiritual discernment.

Zeal, represented by the disciple Simon the Zealot (also known as the Canaanite), is also closely related to the powers of faith and strength. Simon, if you recall, was the original name of Peter, the disciple of faith. The name *Simon*, metaphysically, means "spiritual substance," and faith is the power to shape substance. So zeal is the power to have intense faith and to shape substance with great ardor—all the more reason for the cooling effects of wisdom, of spiritual discrimination!

Zeal: A Fuel for Spiritual Pioneering

Christopher H. Jackson

For many years now I have been pondering just how spirituality will evolve during the age that is before us. One realization constantly coming to me is that it is ultimately impossible to do more than speculate about the future. We all operate out of the human tendency to predict future events out of the context of past and present experience. I am no exception to the human condition. If it were one way yesterday and another way today, I could use my intellect and logic to say that it will likely be a certain way tomorrow. But part of exploring spirituality is the recognition that Spirit is not bound by precedent. We are changing the context out of which we interpret the experience of living. That's why the twenty-first century may well be the most exciting and simultaneously frightening era that has ever been.

We are in the midst of a massive, fundamental *paradigm shift*. In other words, we are in the process of redefining all the assumptions we have ever made about ourselves, other people, and life itself. People everywhere are discovering that the old rules no longer apply. Ideas and precepts that have been taken for granted for centuries are now being challenged, and humanity is being invited to experience a new way of living—one in which even our most cherished beliefs are being allowed to change according to our understanding in *any given moment.*

Spirituality in the twenty-first century is not about absolutes. It is, rather, about evolution. As each of us shares from our momentary revelation, we become a support group for the entire human family. As we share individual perspectives openly and honestly, unafraid of being "right" or "wrong" in our analysis, we unconsciously give others permission to do the same. We begin to recognize that we are all pioneers moving through the realm of unexplored possibilities. No one of us has all the answers. Together, however, we can synergistically uncover truths about life that support us in moving forward—allowing us to become increasingly aware of the natural momentum of all of life—and cooperate with it. It's no longer about any one of us discovering the Truth and then benevolently passing it on to others. We are each discovering that we are a guru ourselves, and that we can combine our exceptional and often highly diverse spiritual insights into a conglomerate which illumines our way one step further into the great mystery of life.

It's not about whether or not my observations in this chapter contain ultimate Truth—it is only about what thoughts and revelations they stir in your own mind as part of your discovery of your own truth. Perhaps, then you will share your revelation with another, and the process will continue.

THE COSMIC CONSPIRACY

One of the most exciting discoveries of the third millennium will be a new way of life, one that is more than a chaos of successes and failures. It'll be a life greater than a coincidental series of circumstances that you and I must clumsily adapt to. *The Force that created us knows what it is doing.* Behind the apparent entanglements and difficulties of our life there is a cosmic conspiracy unfolding. It's always there—behind our clouded judgments and discomforts—and it can be trusted. In fact, if we are to move gracefully and successfully into an age of spiritual enlightenment, it *must* be trusted.

I am just beginning to glimpse life as a synchronistic, phenomenally orchestrated progression of people and events—each designed to move me into a greater awareness of who I am and why I am on the planet. I have never known so little and yet been so filled with joyous anticipation.

THE DIVINE AGENDA

I am daily realizing that life is not driven by my own personal agenda and desired outcomes. I don't know what is best for me or anyone else. Buckminster Fuller once said that human beings are the only species ever to occupy Earth which was presumptuous enough to think it was in charge.

Whether you find it frightening or freeing, you're not in charge of life! To the contrary, life is in charge of you! You will always be happier and more fulfilled in your endeavors if you are willing to release your personal ideals and goals in order to make way for the divine agenda in your life.

Humanity has long lived in the comfortable confines of a defined life. Most of us think we know how life "should" be, and we feel quite justified in our efforts to convince others that our way is the right way. This seems matter-of-fact when we are engaged in simple interaction with one or two other people. Taken to the extreme, however, it is the stuff that wars are made of and the cause of the death of millions—in everything from holy wars to the Holocaust.

The divine agenda doesn't depend on personal judgments—there is no principle of right and wrong or good and bad. There is only the constant, age-old evolution of life under the steady direction of the creative force. Deep into our DNA this evolutionary unfoldment is encoded within us, and we experience it as our own deepest Truth. It's a truth that will never be found in the dictates we receive from people or belief structures found outside of us. It is only tapped when we release what we have been told our life "should" be and open ourselves to the field of unexplored possibilities from which all of life moves forward.

When we stand as spiritual pioneers on the threshold of the realm of unexplored possibilities, we are ready to accept whatever life brings to us and recognize it as our next step toward growth in the divine agenda. We can finally stop trying to control our lives and allow the divine agenda to have its way with us. We can start to trust our life as part of something great and grand that is moving us just where we need to be.

Recently a friend pointed out the superiority of humans over the plant and wildlife kingdoms. Another friend quickly responded by saying that the exact reverse was true. "Plants and wildlife know how to allow," she said, "while humans know only how to control. Allowing is a higher way of living than controlling." *Controlling* is an old paradigm concept, I later thought to myself. It is connected to a life driven by one's personal agenda. *Allowing* is a new paradigm concept, wherein we trust the divine agenda enough to allow its natural influence over our life.

ZEAL: THE FUEL OF EVOLUTION

The cosmic drama of our life is always showing—at a theatre in you, as you. Each frame moves you out of one way of being and into another. The evolution of life is an Academy Award-winning presentation. It is produced, powered, and fueled by an amazing energy described by Unity co-founder Charles Fillmore as "zeal."

Like the current of a river, the fuel of zeal drives us across the waters of the cosmos and through the twists and turns of our individual life path. It is withheld only momentarily by our own resistance, just long enough to build up a force that forges its way onward. The energy of zeal propels a continous momentum of change, for always the waters of the river are changing and new. The goal is always the same, to invest in the flow of the current, rather than in resisting it.

Moving into the third millennium, the energy of zeal is more accessible to you and me than ever before. It requires only that we be willing to move our attention away from holding on and direct it toward letting go.

In the years ahead you may find that your long-held attempts to impede change in your life are failing. Hesitant to trust the always changing river of life, you may find yourself investing your zealous energy in your own personal agenda and desires. Now is the time to recognize the divine agenda at work in your life and cooperate with it as fully as possible.

Letting Go

One of the favorite lesson topics in Unity's popular devotional magazine *Daily Word* is "Let Go, Let God." It's no wonder. People know they are designed to let go and trust life, but they have forgotten how. We all want to be reminded of how we are intended to live.

How do we let go? We begin to recognize life as a process of continuous change. We observe that human beings are magnificently designed to adapt to change—in fact, it is our very nature, what we are designed to do! Change is natural and life-giving. It is the misperception of change as something to be avoided and feared that brings resistance and stagnation.

We have wanted the experiences of yesterday and today to be the experiences of tomorrow. We have wanted to employ the same assumptions and core beliefs we held in the past to serve us in the present and into the future. If we could just hold on to the way things were yesterday, we would not have to fear what they might become tomorrow. So we have enthusiastically held on to old ways of living, trying endlessly to make them applicable to our lives today. The millennium won't hear of this, and more importantly, neither will you—in the deepest essence of who you are.

Nature will move forward, and being one with nature, we will go along for the ride—regardless of our personal preferences. We have tried hard to believe that we could control life, other people, institutions, and even nature. We believed that if we could somehow freeze life, we could control it. One way or another, though, the zealous current will have its way. I believe the twenty-first century will make it quite obvious that we are not in charge of life. Quite the contrary, life is most definitely in charge of us.

Our discovery will be a great one. You see, while we may not be able to trust our own personal agenda in life, we can more than ever trust the divine agenda. God as life has been busy moving and shaping in the evolutionary process for countless millennia, and this current moment is no exception. You and I are here for a precious while, but the whole of life (as God) moves powerfully and enthusiastically in eternity.

XII

109

XXI

YOU HAVE A CHOICE

Charles Fillmore reminded us that zeal is no respecter of persons. It will work on behalf of anyone who employs it for any reason. So, he says, we must exercise both wisdom and love in its use. Here is the key to the power of zeal. In wisdom and in love, begin to get excited about where the river of life, the divine agenda, is moving you. Be willing to release the status quo and its promise of comfort and security. Do what you were created to do—trust life! Trust the force that created you. Trust the force that has provided for you from the very beginning. Modeling all of nature around you, start allowing the flow of life in *your* life. Stop toiling in stressful and futile efforts to be the same person in the same world you were yesterday. Use the energy of life, the zeal of your life, to propel you magnificently forward instead of holding tightly to the place where you are right now.

A few years ago I made a trek to a local water park with my family. As we enjoyed all the wet, watery attractions, I kept noticing the huge water slide at the top of the hill. Though I was fearful, the adventure kept calling to me, and I finally entered a waiting line of people, mostly much younger and more daring than I am, who wanted to take the plunge. Waiting and climbing up several flights of stairs to the top of the slide, I noticed that my fear seemed to grow.

When I finally arrived at the top, I sat down in a basin with several streams of cold water that made the slide slippery enough to move me down at what seemed like the speed of light. A large wooden rail was in front of me. While it was in place, I could cling securely to it. Then suddenly, the operator pushed a button and the rail slipped aside. I was free to launch myself. I took a breath and pushed forward. I didn't move. The operator looked down at me somewhat puzzled. "Sir," she said, "if you want to go anywhere, you will have to let go." At that point I glanced down to see that, while I was continuing to push myself down the slide, my fingers were tightly grasping the side rails of the slide in a manner which made sure I was going nowhere.

I wanted to move forward but my fear of plummeting downward kept me unconsciously clinging tightly. I realized the operator was right. If I wanted to go anywhere, I would have to let go. After one more massive breath, I uncurled my fingers and sped down the slide.

The sensation was incredible. I felt wonderfully alive. I found myself trusting the slide, the water, and the gravity. It was wonderfully exhilarating, and when I at last was submerged in the pool below, I wanted to ride again . . . and again.

PRESERVATION OR PIONEERING?

How many times I have thought of those words: "If you want to go anywhere, you will have to let go"! And this is so true of life. If we want to go anywhere in life, we must find the courage to overcome the erroneous idea that our adventure cannot be trusted. We must reinvest our zealous energy from clinging to soaring. In that bold change we will find life to be wonderfully exhilarating.

As the twenty-first century becomes a living reality, you and I will have a choice, as we always do in life. How do we want to use the power of zeal? We can invest it in becoming a preserver, holding tightly and sometimes painfully to old ways of living and being, or we can invest it in becoming a pioneer, ever seeking the new way of life that is just over the next horizon.

I believe that the third millennium is the dawning of the age of spiritual pioneerism. I believe that people everywhere are experiencing personal life dramas and decisions which are encouraging them to let go of long-held, even "sacred" ways of living. For those who are able to transfer their enthusiasm from clinging to soaring, the realm of unexplored life possibilities will be ecstatic. As in my slippery adventure, once we have let go of a long-held belief about ourselves or other people that no longer serves us, we slide into a new belief. We allow ourselves to flow freely with the constant river of evolution and change called "life." It is unquestionably a state of bliss.

PUNISHMENT OR PARADISE?

In keeping with the dualistic nature of all physical life, the third millennium will find us dealing with two forces, both of which are necessary and neither of which needs to be judged by the other. There will be the preservers, who invest their zeal in maintaining the way things have been. From this fervent crowd we will hear the admonition to stay firmly entrenched in the old ways or face a wrath of punishment ranging from floods and famines to plagues and prophecies of doom. There will be the pioneers, who invest their zeal in the promise of how things can be. These soldiers will be marching rapidly, professing a brighter tomorrow with promises of a new species of universal human and final freedom from the chains of limited thinking. It is somewhere between these two extremes that life will move onward as it is so magnificently designed to do!

The key here involves not so much balance as what author and spiritualist Walter Starcke calls "integration." It is those who hold this realization that will make the greatest contributions in the days ahead—those of us who can embrace the value of the assumptions, beliefs, and ways of being that have brought us this far and yet maintain a vision of how life can brilliantly evolve in the future.

When I first began to realize this process in my own life, being quite aware of my own compulsive and excessive nature, I swung to the extreme of the pioneer—wanting to forge ahead without much regard for the past. By stepping too far, too fast, I learned the folly of both ends of the pendulum. Now I am learning to reach for the future out of the glorious past and the exquisite present moment.

Breaking Through or Breaking Down?

The futurist and spiritual teacher Barbara Marx Hubbard articulates the perceptive ability we have to observe not only that which is breaking *down* around us, but that which is breaking *through* before us. Because of the progressive and evolutionary nature of life, *there is always something breaking through that which is breaking down.*

So what does it mean to be a spiritual pioneer at the dawn of the third millennium? It means to ground yourself solidly in the reality of your present moment, while keeping your vision on the unexplored possibilities over the horizon of the future. The ground beneath your feet supports you completely, but it does not keep you from taking your next step.

Let's look at a few arenas of life to examine this concept more closely. Once you see how it works in a few life situations, you'll begin to use it everywhere. After some time, your vision will be less fixed on what is breaking down in your life and more expansive in terms of what is breaking through.

NEW MODELS FOR RELATIONSHIPS

I have learned about this one from firsthand experience, as I'm sure many of you have. I mention this arena first because so many people are experiencing major changes in their relationships with other people. The models of lover, wife, husband, family, "significant other," partner, and friend are all changing in incredible ways, for as much as we enjoyed the excitement in the drama of passionate romance and the stability of blood relation, these models are giving way to something infinitely greater.

Relationship is being redefined as the creation of a safe space between two people in which roles, including everything from social expectations and obligation to family-focused morals, are de-emphasized. Rather than a commitment to each other, the commitment is to the revelation of self through the other person. Does this sound selfish? Just remember that Jesus told us to love ourselves as we love our neighbors. How can you love someone you do not know? As we find ourselves in other people, by relating with honesty, compassion, and love, we make the only real, possible relationship happen.

It's a relationship not based on expectation. We're not in it to try to make the other person do anything. We are simply present in the other person's life to serve as a mirror. In this way, we give each other the greatest of all gifts—the gift of acceptance and the revelation of self. We are also recognizing that we are members of a community greater than our immediate family—we are all kin to one another in the family of humanity.

It's a whole new ball game. It's as though we are growing out of our prom-years puberty and into a more mature awareness of love, relationship, commitment, family, and community.

Now, instead of being aghast at the next divorce statistic you hear, just remember that some current and long-standing social forms for relationships are being shaken up so that the human family can explore its kinship in new and different ways. Trust what Life is doing in the arena of relationships, and expect to find new, effective frameworks in which your relationships with other people can thrive.

In 1996 I ended an eighteen-year marriage. The process took me three years. Why so long? Well, while my relationship to my partner seemed to satisfactorily fulfill the requirements of traditional matrimony, it refused to be packaged in any established social construct—including marriage. Out of our great love, shared spiritual quests, and commitment to our children, we struggled fervently to maintain ourselves in traditional husband and wife roles. For three years we bent, folded, stapled, and mutilated our relationship in an effort to make it fit.

It took a long time for me to realize that the cosmic connection I shared with my partner had outgrown the social institution. Once freed from it in divorce, it would be able to express itself freely and spontaneously. It would be based on loving desire, rather than obligatory instruction. Does this mean that everyone needs a divorce in the new millennium? No, it means only that we must be willing to let go of relationship frameworks from the past if and when the current of life is moving our relationship into a different form of expression.

In what ways do you see relationships changing in your world? What are your current criteria for family, friendship, community, and partnership? What is breaking through in relationships and what is breaking down? There are no right and wrong answers here. The emergence of your deeper Self will tell you what is right for you, and it will respect and care for you and all others in your life as well. This leads us to the next arena of change for the twenty-first century—religion.

RELIGION FOR A NEW MILLENNIUM

I once heard someone say, "You must believe in God, in spite of everything the clergy tells you about Him!" To this, I wholeheartedly add, we must believe in our spirituality in spite of our religion! I am hard pressed to defend one religious belief over another. If I advocate any position on this, it's that the only valid religion is the religion of you. We've tried worshiping the sacred quality of everybody and everything except ourselves! Why not dare to believe that *each unique, incredible soul on the planet has his or her own religion.* This is not a religion of the written word, except as it is written on the heart of every person. We are all walking different ways on the same path. Let us honor that what is right and wrong and good and bad for one person is not the same for another. With self-acceptance and respect and mutual compassion, we can follow our path with absolute certainty that it will not violate the path of another.

Philosopher and student Andrew Harvey has purported that the new millennium will find us abandoning idols of worship in all their forms. The new worship will be that of recognition of the divine in all persons and in all of life. Every moment of this precious awareness will be a sacred prayer of humility and thanksgiving.

Our church will become our daily life—for at last religion and our daily life are becoming one. Andrew Harvey was for years a close affiliate of Mother Meera, the sage mentor of a great following of devotees. After serving for a lengthy time as her personal spokesperson, Harvey announced his desire for a same-sex union. Disillusioned by Meera's apparent admonition that Harvey reject a gay lifestyle and pursue a member of the opposite sex, he left her as his guru. The sequence of events surrounding his disclosure led Harvey to a recognition of his own, internal divine guidance system. He began to trust himself and his own life more than anyone or anything else. Today, he declares his freedom from the worship of anything outside of his own, internal divinity and integrity.

The religion of the twenty-first century is the recognition that in our frail and weary human form there is something incredibly divine. It has been there all along, but we were dreaming, with eyes that looked outward, instead of awakening, with inner vision.

As we shine the light of honesty on ourselves, we begin to find a confidence and power that brings all parts of ourselves to life. From such a grand vantage point, we are able to start giving the gift of our newly discovered selves to the world. As people bring their wholeness to life, behold—the world itself is made whole. What a mighty and worthy religion is the acceptance, nurturing, and love of Self! It inevitably shines outward to become the stuff with which the world will be saved.

Work Communities for the Twenty-First Century

Being part of a large religious bureaucracy has afforded me the opportunity to make some interesting observations about twenty-first–century life in the workplace. Long-held concepts about leaders and followers are giving way to a more community-oriented concept of corporate structure. Presidents and chairpersons are now adapting to new definitions of their roles as facilitators rather than directors. There is new awareness in traditional corporate structure that is based on this concept: *While we are not the same, we are equal.*

The success of any corporate endeavor depends significantly on each individual contribution, and everything from parts placement to strategic planning is enhanced through involvement at every organizational level.

As with all the changes resulting from redefinition, leaders who have found power in their titles and unchallenged authority are, sometimes uncomfortably, being forced to lead, with honest disclosure of their fears and insecurities. Perhaps they no longer have all the solutions to the challenges their organizations face; perhaps they never really did. Perhaps they must recognize that such answers must now be derived from the "group think" of every individual they employ. An organization is, after all, no less than the sum total of each person who makes up the enterprise.

A new level of performance can be found by leaders who recognize their role as facilitators of the incredible creativity and zealous energy that is available when all members of an organization are recognized for their unique contributions, skills, and abilities. New organizational vision can be mined and shared from this perspective.

For many years in my management career, I believed that, as a leader, I was supposed to be a fountain of ideas, solutions, and vision. My primary role was to create the vision and pass it downward into the organization.

Obviously, while I still hold my own ideas and vision for Unity, I am increasingly aware of the group consciousness of every individual who has ever been or is now a part of this movement. This consciousness has its own life and momentum. My role as a leader is not to impose my vision upon the Unity movement, but to recognize the organization's natural momentum and support it whenever my internal and intuitive nature identifies it at work.

Awkwardly, this means I may not always know where the movement is going. Assuredly, it also means that I can move with this natural momentum *one step at a time* and trust it completely. It is a new, far more inclusive manner of leadership, and it is worthy of experimentation in any corporate or organizational setting.

Honoring Ourselves

The new millennium may find us engaged in the art of becoming more perfectly human. A true model of the spiritual pioneer, Walter Starcke, has observed that our humanity is our divinity in disguise. Especially amongst New Thought groups, this realization can be immensely refreshing.

Throughout human history we have been engaged in an attempt to "overcome" our humanity and attain our divinity. Even the Unity movement has been about overcoming. How many times have I heard Unity students lament the inherent difficulty of trying to overcome their human frailties in order to become the Christ? To that endeavor I now respond by saying, "Why not accept and love who you are—faults and frailties, vices and virtues." My colleague and friend Jim Rosemergy calls this accepting the "sacred human."

The path of the spiritual pioneer is one of acceptance. If we are striving to become the Divine in physical expression, why not begin by emulating the qualities of that Divine, whatever we may perceive them to be? We know that the Divine is not about judgment and condemnation, so let's cease demonstrating those qualities in our own lives, beginning first with our own humanity. God is love, and love is the absence of judgment of good and bad and right and wrong. Love is acceptance. Love is kindness.

Can we begin to accept ourselves—especially those parts of ourselves that we have been told are unacceptable? Can we reach out to those supposedly despicable aspects of our human nature and gently embrace them and lead them into the light for healing? Yes, we can. We can redirect the zealous energy of our life from self-condemnation to self-acceptance. We can decide that, regardless of what we have been told about ourselves in the past, we are lovable. In fact, we are the beloved of our Creator. We are worthy. We are capable. We are divine creations, just the way we are right now!

LIVING FROM MOMENT TO MOMENT

People often ask me how to live in the moment. I begin with the recognition that I have lived, historically, and even for the most part today, outside of the moment. I have interpreted most of my reality from the way my life has been or how I thought it would or should be in the future.

A good friend and counselor once encouraged me to follow this framework:

1. Admit that I do not know what is best for me or how my life "should" be.
2. Acknowledge my feelings, my thoughts, and my intuitive impulses in this present moment. Be willing to let them lead me, collectively, as my guides on the path of the spiritual pioneer.
3. Visualize a blank computer screen in my mind.
4. Trust that, as I let go of previously prescribed solutions and open myself to what is in this present moment, I will be shown my next step on the screen in my mind.
5. Ask the universe to provide me with whatever clarification or further instruction I believe I need. Be willing to find the courage to follow the guidance I receive. Be willing to release my personal agenda and cooperate with the divine agenda, or the current of the river of life.

Is this easy? For myself, not really. It is a new way of living. I may be awkward and clumsy at first. I may look foolish. Like anything new, it requires that I be gentle with my learning curve and be willing to make mistakes. But I will eventually master it—just as I have mastered the old ways of living.

In time I will become more and more comfortable and secure operating from this new vantage point. I will increasingly acknowledge the benefits and find more peace and fulfillment in my life. I will discover a refreshingly new and more spiritually evolved manner of living that will serve me as I cross over the threshold of a new century, a new millennium. It will serve me well until it is time to let it go—time for yet a newer way of being, a newer age—for life is lived in eternity and I pray that I may ever change and be made new with each step onward.

Christopher H. Jackson is, along with Jim Rosemergy, executive vice president of Unity School of Christianity at Unity Village, Missouri. He has enjoyed a lifelong affiliation with Unity and has worked at the Village for over twenty years.

Chris has spoken at Unity gatherings throughout the United States and Europe. His writings have been featured in *Daily Word*, a magazine that reaches out to people of all faiths and serves more than a million subscribers. At Unity School, his work includes guiding Silent Unity, which is one of the oldest international prayer ministries and which responds to more than two million requests for prayer support annually.

Chris is the author of the audiocassette programs, *Healing Your Mind, Healing Your Heart: How Spiritual Healing Can Transform Your Life,* and *A Path to Peace: Finding Inner Peace in Daily Life.*

CHAPTER VII

THE POWER OF STRENGTH

"As soon as they left the synagogue, they entered the house of Simon and Andrew, with James and John. Now Simon's mother-in-law was in bed with a fever, and they told him about her at once. He came and took her by the hand and lifted her up. Then the fever left her, and she began to serve them. That evening, at sundown, they brought to him all who were sick or possessed with demons. And the whole city was gathered around the door. And he cured many who were sick with various diseases, and cast out many demons; and he would not permit the demons to speak, because they knew him."

—Mark 1:29–34

A quick metaphysical interpretation of this Scripture would tell us the following: The partnership of faith and strength (Simon Peter and Andrew) can lead to imbalance (the mother-in-law's fever) and is aided by the powers of wisdom and love (James and John). Jesus, who does the healing, represents the Christ, the One Power, the perfect harmony of all the twelve powers. This healing draws out all imbalance everywhere and brings harmony to all.

Of course, there is also a hint of zeal in the brothers Simon and Andrew as well as in the fever. When faith and strength combine, zeal is a natural outgrowth. Excess zeal is healed by bringing to it the awareness of spiritual discernment and love. When healed, excess zeal can offer its enthusiasm as service to the other powers. This enables the powers of faith and strength to become an enduring consciousness of health and vitality. Driven by the grace of the Christ wholeness, this consciousness of balanced strength is so powerful that it draws to it all which is out of alignment, all which is in need of healing, and all are healed.

Andrew represents the power of strength, and he is the brother of Simon Peter. In balance with the other powers of faith, wisdom, and love, strength avoids the excess of zeal and becomes a stable force that sustains life and consciousness.

Finding Strength in Our Brokenness

Bernie Siegel, M.D.

Claude Bernard said, "I have the conviction that when physiology will be far enough advanced the poet, the philosopher, and the physiologist will all understand each other." As we begin to see strength in much broader terms than simply as a physical condition, an emotional attribute, or a mental virtue, then we discover what it really is. Strength is a spiritual quality that goes much deeper than the body—and it positively and dramatically affects the body when we make it a way of life.

Ernest Hemingway wrote, "The world breaks everyone, and afterward many are strong at the broken places." This truth is difficult for most of us to accept. We focus on the brokenness and never take notice that we have become stronger at the broken places. Yes! When fractures heal, they become stronger than the bone. Nature teaches us a principle in the body that is also true in the soul—that pain is a teacher, protector, and definer of one's self. It's a difficult message and one from which we usually try to escape. As a culture we are willing to go to almost any length to numb and distract ourselves from feeling our pain. Just watch television for a few hours, and you will be informed about every over-the-counter painkiller known to man. Is this a healthy practice—one that creates strength? No, I don't think so. Becoming stronger isn't about finding easy solutions to every difficulty or cures for every illness. It is about facing difficulties with grace and presence. We need our pain to protect, teach, and define ourselves.

In the new millennium, it will be time to reopen the study of healing by changing its focus. Those who will not only survive but thrive will have strengthened themselves by turning their attention from disease and death to health and life. In the practice of medicine as a whole, we will not move forward until we have made this same kind of change in theory and in practice. When the practice of medicine becomes primarily about healing rather than curing, it will then be about creating and building strength, rather than simply curbing and avoiding weakness. Every generation has and always will have its threatening illnesses. If we find a cure for one, then another takes its place. If we find a wonder drug for one, then we must search for another wonder drug for the next. We need therefore to focus not just on finding new wonder drugs, but on learning how to utilize the naturally occurring "wonder drugs" that exist within each of us. I predict that within the next decade, through genetic engineering, these internal wonder drugs will be produced and used therapeutically. How much better it will be when we stop waiting on science to validate our natural, God-given healing powers and, rather, allow science to teach us that we can be our own genetic engineers, creating and developing strength through our own inner abilities!

Pain as a Teacher

My friend Max Cleland, author of *Strong at the Broken Places,* is a United States Senator from Georgia. Max is also a triple amputee, his limbs a casualty of a grenade explosion. Sue Ann Easely from Alabama is a cancer patient and has a debilitating case of athetoid cerebral palsy. Despite her inability to control the movement of her limbs, she personally typed her autobiography: *The Bird With the Broken Wing.* Sue Ann's nurse tied her into her wheelchair and gagged her so she wouldn't drool; then Sue Ann typed the 250-page manuscript with her nose! The weakness in her body was no match for the strength in her soul! So, who are the strong? Those who have strong bodies, good fortune, and no pain? No, the strong are those who know how to deal with difficulties and continue to be fully alive.

Why is pain necessary? What do we need to understand about pain—about its role and its ability to enhance our spiritual development? Dr. Jean Houston, noted anthropologist and psychologist, observes, "Illness opens the doors to a reality which is closed to a healthy point of view." Pain is a teacher that can focus our attention, push us to move beyond our mental/emotional limitations, and ultimately bring us closer to God. Pain helps us to discover our authentic selves and to define our purpose. It also indicates where we need to protect ourselves. Clarissa Pinkola Estes tells a story about how pain can break us from a tangle of immobilizing thinking in our lives. In the story, the narrator comes upon a pile of boys all tangled together and lying in the snow. When asked why they don't get up and go home to get warm, they say, "We're all tangled and afraid to move. We might break an arm or leg. We can't tell what belongs to each of us."

Our storyteller then says, "I can help," and proceeds to take one boy's gloves off. Then she jabs his hand. When he yelps, she replies, "That's your hand; now move it!" By repeating this process, each boy is, in turn, untangled.

We need our pain to define and protect ourselves. When people develop neuropathies and lose the ability to feel pain, they lose those parts of their bodies that they can't protect. When you lose touch with your feelings and emotions, both painful and pleasant, you cannot respond properly to life. Acknowledging and responding to our pain is a path to healing. Reacting to our pain by anesthetizing it robs us of its gift—its capacity to bring us to wholeness. Strength comes from using the pain and learning from it.

I saw a slogan on a T-shirt that said, "It's never too late to have a happy childhood." As children, most of us did not grow up in an environment with sufficient love and hope. We are born with an innate awareness of our strength, but often those first authorities in our lives—parents, caregivers, teachers, clergy—weaken us with mistaken attitudes and misguided rules. Guilt, shame, and blame drain us of our strength and separate us from the reservoirs of strength within us, so that they may go untapped for years or perhaps our entire lives. Although each of us is an incredible child of God and begins life with great potential, two-thirds of us have either contemplated or attempted suicide by the time we finish high school. Few of us are trained to use our inner skills to deal effectively with life. To become strong, we must move beyond that legacy of lovelessness, to forgive, and to be reborn.

We are so out of tune with our inner strength that we are no better at handling good fortune than bad fortune. Ninety-five percent of lottery winners say winning ruined their lives. Once, at a conference, I asked the question, "Is life fair?" and heard the loudest and most emphatic response I have ever received. "No!" You might have thought that I was addressing oncology patients or advocates for the homeless or some other group who were dealing with major misfortunes in life. This was the Young Presidents Organization, a group usually considered to have succeeded in the pursuit of the American dream.

When we understand that life is difficult, not unfair, then we can learn to deal with the difficulties and make life easier for ourselves and others. We need to cultivate courage in the face of our fears, become fully present with our pain, so that we can learn the unique message it has for us and allow it to strengthen us. That is how we become strong. We fear the pressure that pain puts on us to grow, but we forget it's a natural part of the process. Charcoal is hardly regarded as a valuable or beautiful gem, but when placed under tremendous pressure, that's exactly what it becomes—a diamond.

When we allow the pressure of pain to create diamonds in us, then we can express our compassion for others, serve instead of waiting to be served, and become like angels in disguise. With this knowledge and work, comes a strength born of love. We then will fear nothing and will be able to endure anything.

I'd like to give you a personal example. I have had three problems over the past few years. My wife Bobbie and I frequently travel to speak. I love to run and train for marathons. I have recently participated in five of them, and all of this creates a very busy life. So what does God produce in my body?

1. Laryngitis, which forces me to shut down.
2. Tendon and bone injuries in my feet, which forces me to slow down. And if I don't get the message . . .
3. Vertigo, which forces me to lie down.

So intense is my enthusiasm for running marathons that my body has to respond with extreme symptoms to get my attention. After watching this series of illnesses become a pattern in my life, I began to take notice. I've learned to listen to my body. Carl Jung said, "Analysis is like surgery without anesthesia." The people who respond to psychotherapy, studies show, are the people who become aware of the feelings that exist in their bodies. They have the strength to sustain wounds, which opens their hearts and minds. They are strengthened and healed by this experience.

For me the true test of strength is our ability to accept our mortality and live a full life with death as our teacher. As a physician working with cancer patients, I have seen that when people truly find the strength to live in the face of life-threatening illnesses, they frequently don't die as predicted by their doctors and by medical statistics. They teach us about survival and the inner qualities that go with it. Accepting our mortality—using it as a motivator and not denying it, looking into the shadows of our unconscious, developing self-love and self-esteem—this is how we heal our lives and strengthen our souls. True healers know the value of afflictions and adversity. They know that within the symbolic experience of disease lies a path to change and self-healing.

Years ago I wrote about a patient of mine who was a doctor. His parents had put tremendous pressure on him to become a doctor, and so he had given in and abandoned his dream of being a violinist. He was later diagnosed with an inoperable brain tumor and given, at best, a year to live. He accepted the diagnosis and said, "Well, if I've only got a year to live I'm going to play the violin," and he did. A year later he was a violinist in the city orchestra and had no brain tumor.

I could tell you many, many stories like this, all true, of patients who have been strengthened and healed through the lessons of their pain. They accepted their mortality, allowed their pain to awaken them to the ways in which they were not pursuing their joy, and then made the commitment to begin really living. No matter what our problems may be, we can learn from the wounded about survival, about the importance of self-esteem, and about our ability to dramatically change our beliefs about ourselves. We will learn that we can learn, grow, and live fully at any ending stage.

USE EVERYTHING TO GET WELL

We will also learn about the importance of God and how the truly strong give their problems to God. It is not a sign of weakness to turn to God and family, but rather, one of ultimate wisdom and strength. The strong know it is appropriate and even necessary to ask for help, and they are not afraid of rejection. Strength lies in the ability to ask boldly and give people freedom to accept or refuse, including yourself. The strong have no trouble saying no to things they don't want to do, and out of love, they will do things that would wear other people out. They know that life is a labor pain and that they are giving birth to themselves. They know the importance of support and love in reducing the pain. They also choose which pains to experience in order to give birth to themselves.

If you are acting out of love, your body is physiologically as healthy as it can be and is as strong as it will ever be. The same is true for those who receive unconditional love.

When you are loving, you literally don't feel pain. From the impressive display of a mother cat rescuing five kittens from a burning building to a human mother lifting a car off her child, we can see the strength of love and its ability to eliminate pain more powerfully than any pill or injection.

There is a painting I love called *The Consultation*. In it a sick woman lies in a hospital bed surrounded by a nurse, doctor, and medications. A Christlike figure appears in the painting. I wish her family could be in the picture too. The strong use everything in the picture to get well. You and God are a team, and your family is a player as well. It isn't wrong to use medications, but they are helpers, not solutions.

XII

129

XXI

A RESPONSIBLE COCREATOR

Each of us has moments when we ask: "Why is pain necessary? If God is truly good, why didn't God create a world free of problems, diseases, difficulties, and suffering?" I believe it is so that we can be cocreators, cultivate strength, and demonstrate compassion. I believe the concept of a "perfect" world free of problems is a gimmick, a magic trick, and a scenario that leaves us with no role and no meaning to our lives. We are cocreators, and it takes a great deal of strength and work to be a conscious cocreator. To choose God's way, the way of peace, in the midst of adversity takes incredible strength and points us to the source of strength—unlimited love.

In the story "The Grand Inquisitor" by Fyodor Dostoevsky, the Inquisitor tells the Christlike prisoner that his captors will burn and torture him tomorrow. When he is finished, the Inquisitor waits for the prisoner to rage at him and fight back, but the prisoner walks forward and silently kisses him on his aged lips. The Inquisitor then suddenly realizes his own tremendous weakness, the poison in his soul, and he is transformed by the incredible demonstration of strength and love shown by his prisoner. The Inquisitor then opens the prisoner's cell and releases him.

A Unity minister once had her purse taken by a man with a ski mask on. She said, "I know behind that mask is someone you could love." He dropped her purse and ran. Years later, a man approached her in church and admitted he was the masked thief. He then thanked her for changing his life. Of course, *she* didn't change his life; *he* did. Knowing that he was loved gave him the strength to do it.

I can share other stories, some from my own life, that are similar. It takes strength, presence of mind, and a commitment to be a responsible cocreator, to be loving in situations where rage and resentment are more common. If love does not appear to work immediately, you have not failed. Remember Jeremiah watching the potter work the clay. You mustn't give up or fail, but instead start again and re-create until you are satisfied with the result. Life is a process, and one in which the truly strong understand the need for reshaping their lives by continually forgiving self and others.

We know how easy it is to be addicted, to never exercise, to eat unhealthy foods, and so on. It takes strength and love to discipline yourself. When the insight comes to you, the inner vision of how very precious you are to God, and you understand why you were created, then you find the strength to begin to truly live a life of love.

If you are fortunate, you have parents who teach, coach, and set an example for you. For most this is not the case. Some of our early teachers weakened us with their fears, rules, and obstacles. I feel very fortunate to have had parents who had the strength to love without conditions and who helped me make decisions based upon my feelings. I had parents who taught me that adversity is God's redirection from which something good will come. The practice of that insight—that all adversity is a redirection from God, that God's will of good is always at work, even when it does not seem so—is what we call "faith." Faith is the rich soil of the soul in which even the tiniest seed of strength will grow. It will continue to grow until it is a predominant trait within us and then a permanent principle by which we live our lives. A life lived in faith brings with it a peace and a strength that is not attainable in other ways.

THE SCIENCE BEHIND THIS

Let me stop for a moment to discuss the science behind this. Our body chemistry is altered by our thoughts and acts. Whatever you expect, whatever you anticipate, is changing you before the event ever occurs. If it is despair, then it weakens your immune system and you suffer the consequences. Research with college students and actors has shown that changes occur in their hormones, neuropeptides, and immune systems when they anticipate joy or have a joyful role to play, versus anticipating fear or playing a tragic role. If love, hope, and faith flourish in your mind, your body benefits from chemistry that strengthens you and helps you resist disease and survive tragic events. Science confirms this.

This philosophy of self-healing is not new. It's ancient. It's embodied in the teachings of all the great spiritual masters and teachers. The information about our innate potential to heal, overcome, and strengthen ourselves is all there. My friend and mentor Dr. Karl Menninger stated this clearly in the dedication of his book *Man Against Himself*, published in 1938: "To those who would use intelligence in the battle against death—to strengthen the will to live against the wish to die, and to replace with love the blind compulsion to give hostages to hatred as the price of living."

We have simply lost sight of this truth with our technological orientation. Once, when appearing as a medical expert in a court case relating to stress and illness I was asked, "When did this new theory originate?"

My response was "Hundreds of years ago." Now there are many respected scientists, doctors, and physicists who are giving credence to and proving the existence of our inner abilities to become stronger at the broken places. Physicists have proven to the satisfaction of the scientific community that there is no such thing as a "purely scientific" experiment; in other words, they have proven that the expectations of the experimenter definitely have an effect on the outcome of the experiment. This theory applies just as well, if not more so, to personal and global matters of healing. We can use pain, suffering, and illness to redirect our lives and, in the broadest sense, to heal not just the individual, but society. We now know that illness can be the catalyst for healing and increased love in our personal relationships. In the same way, global "illnesses," like the threat of nuclear disaster, famine, and ecological damage, can lead us to love and healing in our global relationships.

SELF-HEALING IN THE NEW MILLENNIUM

If the outcome of scientific experiments is affected by the attitude of the experimenter, then how much more will the outcome of our own experiments with self-healing and the healing of our world be affected by our attitudes, both positive and negative. Love, hope, joy, and peace of mind have physiological consequences, just as depression and despair do. Although more and more people are coming to believe that the practice of medicine can only assist in healing, rather than cause healing, I believe we will see quantum leaps in the acceptance of self-healing practices in the new millennium. The mind/body medical model, which is proving the reality of self-healing, is becoming more believable to the scientific and medical communities, and at the same time our culture is becoming less reliant upon technology to translate to us the meaning of events in our lives. We are becoming more trusting of our intuition, of our spiritual wisdom, and of our abilities to determine our own level of general health and well-being.

Love is a survival factor for individuals and for our species. So who are the strong? It is not those who can lift the heaviest weights, but those who can carry the greatest burdens with love. Those who can understand, forgive, and love—therein lies true strength. I see myself struggling to be strong as the father of five children, not all of whom think highly of me at any one moment. But I know my role is to love them, and I work at developing the strength to give them the unconditional love that they deserve.

THE ROLES OF LOVE, FAITH, AND HOPE

One of our sons discussed having me as his father when he accompanied me to a meeting where I was to speak to parents of children with cancer. His comments were not all complimentary. When he was done, I agreed with him and hugged him. I received many calls and letters saying that the most important part of the evening was my hugging him and listening to him. It gave other parents the strength to do the same with their children.

I had a great teacher from my own family, someone who demonstrated for me what it means to have the strength to love. Due to complications of my mother's pregnancy, I was born an "ugly duckling." But I wasn't discarded from the nest. My grandmother had the strength to take me and anoint, massage, and love me back to normal. She helped my mother to love me and accept me. Imagine the strength it takes for the mother of an "ugly duckling" to say, "My child is a beautiful child and a gift from God," while the neighbors are staring and whispering!

I do not know any force or power stronger than love. Bombs and weapons cannot equal the force of love. History abounds with tyrants who tried to achieve greatness through force, brutality, and murder. And yet it is the prophets, the lovers, the teachers, and the healers whom we call great.

On a personal note, my journey of strengthening myself has taken me from "our will be done" to "Thy will be done." We might test our level of spiritual strength with this question: If I said, "I want to pray for something for you," what would you ask me to pray for?

If your answer is a personal one—health, money, and so on—then you may want to consider devoting more energy to strengthening yourself spiritually. But if you can sincerely respond with "world peace" or "God's will be done" or "I don't need anything," I'd say you've become a very loving and very strong individual and one I greatly admire. You have transcended personal needs and are truly capable of displaying great strength in the face of adversity. The key to this kind of strength comes from faith. Hope and love in our lives are first cultivated from the seed of faith. Together these can prepare you for any event, no matter how great the burden. I am reminded of a 92-year-old patient of mine who was a member of one of our therapy groups. When the other members of our therapy group were sharing their fears, I asked her what she was most afraid of. She thought a moment and then said, "Driving on the parkway at night!" She had lived through it all in her ninety-two years and knew she had the ability to handle life. She had faith in herself, and it had given her strength to face life's biggest fears with such courage that she no longer concerned herself with them.

Those who have faith cultivate great inner strength and do not fear obstacles. They are redirected by adversity and are open to new directions and possibilities. As Dr. Robert Schuller has said, "Tough times don't last, but tough people do." Norman Vincent Peale's mother gave him great counsel years ago, and it directed him through adversity, into strength, and on to success throughout his life. She said, "Norman, if God slams one door, further down the corridor another will be opened."

When you have strength, you know there is a direction and foundation to your life. You are finished with judgment, regret, and anxiety, and you are busy living. The Talmud tells us, "He who rejoices in the afflictions which are brought upon the self brings salvation to the world." And Psalm 26 appreciates our Creator for giving us strengthening trials: "Prove me, O Lord, and try me; test my heart and mind" (Ps. 26:2).

So, to be of great strength we must have great faith. Then great hope and great love will be woven into the fabric of our lives. These three can provide us with the greatest physical health and strength possible. Science has shown what faith, hope, and love can do for people dealing with life-threatening illnesses. Your body is altered by the peace that comes with this kind of spiritual strength.

Living in faith, hope, and love doesn't mean that we don't have to deal with conflict, fight to make good and appropriate changes, or walk away from those experiences and relationships which are not healthy for us. "The Serenity Prayer" reminds us that there are some things which can't be changed and some which can. What we need is the inner strength to accept what we can't change, the courage to change what we can, and the wisdom to know which is which! This prayer's underlying message is that we are never victims. There is always a healthy, peaceful response to life's challenges, and living in faith, hope, and love directs us to that response. Strength of mind and body comes from that unlimited source which is both within us and around us.

We don't have to know from whence comes our strength. We don't have to understand it or even entirely believe it. We need simply to turn to it by beginning to stretch our faith, by loving beyond our current limits, and by hoping for an outcome that exceeds our expectations. This gives us a strength beyond imagining and one that is available to us no matter what the state of our physical bodies. We are created from Love and will return to Love. Thornton Wilder wrote in *The Bridge of San Luis Rey:*

And we ourselves shall be loved for awhile and forgotten but the love will have been enough. All those impulses of love return to the love that made them. Even memory is not necessary for love. There is a land of the living and a land of the dead and the bridge is love, the only survival, the only meaning.

How do I know this? From personal experience with God. I was jogging down the road on my morning meditation, singing from the old hymn, "I am strong but Thou art weak." I didn't realize what I was singing until that inner voice interrupted me and said: "You've got the words wrong. It's 'Thou art strong but I am weak.'" Then the voice paused and said: "Maybe you are right. I've done such a good job with you that you are truly strong and I don't have to worry about you."

Accept and embrace the strength that is within you. It is yours to discover, to develop, and to enjoy, even though it comes from "God knows where"! As the Bible ends in Revelation, not conclusion, I end with the beginning: Take what you have learned and live a life of faith, love, and strength.

Bernie S. Siegel, M.D., is one of America's most popular holistic physicians. A surgeon, author, and teacher, he has traveled the world giving lectures and workshops.

Bernie has appeared on *Good Morning America*, *The Today Show*, *Phil Donahue*, *Oprah Winfrey*, *Sally Jesse Raphael*, and other television shows. He is the author of numerous articles and three nationally best-selling books: *Love, Medicine and Miracles; Peace, Love and Healing;* and *How to Live Between Office Visits.*

Dr. Siegel received his M.D. from Cornell University and is a past president of the American Holistic Medical Association and a director or advisor for numerous medical boards.

CHAPTER VIII

THE POWER OF WILL

With every urge we have felt to improve ourselves, from losing a few pounds to earning that advanced degree, we conjure up the power of will. We even call it that: willpower!

The power of will is crucial. Similar to wisdom and understanding, both of which exercise the power of discernment, will goes one step further and *acts*. Will is the determining factor. Wisdom and spiritual understanding discriminate between the true and the false—and the will chooses. Will is the executive function, the activator. "You will decide on a matter, and it will be established for you" (Job 22:28).

Also relying heavily on the power of strength, the will is pivotal. Our ability to succeed at meeting our goals depends so much on our capacity to delay gratification. Whether we choose to pursue our sense pleasures or to put them off for a time in favor of a higher cause, we develop our strength of character. In a very real sense, our character then determines who we become.

Matthew (called Levi, son of Alphaeus, in Mark) is the disciple representing will. He was the tax collector who gave much up in order to follow Jesus. In order for our power of will to be surrendered to the Christ, to be willing to do the divine Will, we, too, need to give up our smallness, our selfishness, our ego-fascination with looking good, being right, and controlling the situation. When our will does merge with the divine Will, great advances are made, for we begin to consciously choose the divine way of life. We "repent," to use the old word, we change our life's direction from total absorption in the material world to a growing fascination with matters of the Spirit.

XII
138
XXI

Will: The Foundation Faculty of the New Global Order

Barbara King

"Delighted are those who surrender to God because the sovereign counsel of heaven belongs to them."
—Mt. 5:3 *(the Peshitta, Errico translation)*

As we approach the new millennium, we are finding that the power to create a just, successful, and safe future rests with us and with how we direct our power of will. When we surrender our faith in things, people, institutions (even churches) and surrender our personal will completely to God, we will hear only divine counsel, think only divine ideas, and express ourselves only in divine order. God wants us to be free from the bondage of human will that is marked by force, manipulation, rigidity, and skepticism, in order that we might experience the freedom felt when we completely surrender to the gentle, trusting, all-knowing divine will which is within us.

There is a uniqueness to the power of will. I believe that the key to raising global consciousness is the surrendering of one's personal will to the will of the Higher Consciousness, the Christ Self, or as Dr. Wayne Dyer calls it, "the Sacred Self." When we do this, we will begin to manifest the vision of the millennium which is found in *Webster's* dictionary and which so many of us hold in our hearts:

139

"The thousand years mentioned in Revelation 20 during which holiness is to prevail and Christ is to reign on earth; a period of great happiness or human perfection."

There is a heightened eagerness and a heightened tension running through all of human consciousness as we enter the new millennium. In the next one hundred years we will either sow the seeds of a radical shift towards wholeness and prosperity for everyone or we will play out dramatic scenarios of destruction, injustice, and tyranny—the seeds of which have been sown in this century.

AN OPEN-ENDED POTENTIAL

Dr. Rocco Errico, world scholar in the teachings of the Aramaic language of Jesus, defines *will* in Greek and Aramaic to mean "a wish, desire." God as Father wishes and desires the best for God's children. Jesus the Christ says in the Lord's Prayer, given to the disciples, "Thy will be done on earth as it is in heaven." Our will, directed Godward, is a source of open-ended potential and gives us a heightened sensitivity to and preference for receiving more spiritually than materially.

This potential, properly realized, will enable us to work toward the paradigm of a new consciousness that will change the world and bring us to a global peace and prosperity. All who believe we can make a difference have the opportunity to demonstrate this through *every* level of living and, especially, in their relationships with others. I will use one of the best-loved Bible stories, that of the prodigal son, to illustrate this demonstration. In Luke 15:12–13 (KJV) Jesus tells the story of a father who had two sons:

"And the younger of them said to his father, Father, give me the portion of goods that falleth to me. And he divided unto them his living. And not many days after the younger son gathered all together, and took his journey into a far country, and there wasted his substance with riotous living."

In the East, family property consists of sheep, food, supplies, and a little cash and land. This property does not belong to the father, but to all male members, who have an equal share in it. The firstborn is empowered by his father to act in his absence and to take care of the family. He has the power to buy and sell, receive guests, look after servants and pay them wages, hire and fire laborers, and even punish his mother, brothers, and sisters as he sees fit. Yet, the father chooses to honor the younger son's request for his part of his inheritance. Obviously, this caused jealousy and strained the family's relationships with one another.

Metaphysically, the "younger son" symbolizes one not awakened to his spiritual nature. The "far country" represents being drawn to materialism. The younger son squanders his resources as he takes no responsibility for his livelihood. Sense gratification takes over, and he finds himself hitting rock bottom. He gradually comes to himself and becomes aware of his challenges. He seeks forgiveness by choosing to return home to his father, asking for a position as servant in the household. Even though he has misused his fortune, the father receives him and makes a feast of thanksgiving for the son who was lost and is now found. There is more concerning the elder brother's negative attitude in this story, but I'll stop with the above to share with you how this story and our freedom of choice and spiritual maturity are connected to each other.

In the earlier definitions of the power of will, we clearly see where the younger son got into trouble. His wishes and desires were directed toward sense gratification, rather than spiritual growth, and he directed his power and his unlimited potential selfward and outward rather than Godward. Simply put, he wanted an abun-

XII

141

XXI

dance of worldly wealth, rather than spiritual wealth. The "father" represents the God who wishes and desires the best for us.

MY WILL BE DONE

In the New Testament book of Matthew we find Jesus' only recorded sermon. From 6:24, 31–34 of the Living Bible we read:

> You cannot serve two masters, God and money. For you will love one and hate the other, or else the other way around. So don't worry at all about having enough food and clothing. Why be like the heathen? For they take pride in all these things and are deeply concerned about them. But your heavenly Father already knows perfectly well that you need them, and he will give them to you if you give him first place in your life and live as he wants you to. So don't be anxious about tomorrow. God will take care of your tomorrow too. Live one day at a time.

What does this allegory say about the direction of our personal will? How does this apply to us today, especially to those of us influenced by the "Me" generation? The prodigal son's behavior is that of the limited ego or personality. Arrogance, insensitivity, and self-centeredness are all characteristics of ego behavior and negative emotions. When the thinking and/or feeling nature is connected to the ego, willfulness is the result—"my will be done," rather than "Thy will be done." The behavior of an ego manifests itself on a material level as control, egocentricity, and perfectionism. On an intellectual level, the ego is narrow-minded, lacking in humility, and exclusive. On an emotional level, the ego generates boredom, insensitivity, and repressed feelings. On a spiritual level, the ego has a poverty consciousness and operates from fear, due to its lack of belief in a higher power. It relies completely upon itself to the exclusion of God and others. It sees itself as separate, rather than part of a whole and believes its function is to take and hoard, rather than to give and share.

Take into consideration the morning and late-night talk shows on both radio and television. Americans of every race, culture, and ethnic background are represented. Talk show hosts attempt to do Band-Aid psychology on people suffering from diseased egos, many of whom need extensive therapy and positive role models in their lives. In the same way that the *Leave It to Beaver*-type television shows of the '50s tried to heal the problems of family life in twenty-two minutes of airtime, so current-day talk shows try to acknowledge problems, dialogue viewpoints, and give solutions, all within their allotted time slots. They appear to offer a quick fix to deep-rooted problems, and the prevalence of these types of shows indicates how gullible we are to the illusion of a quick solution to our pain. As I travel nationally and abroad, I find that wherever I go, people are in pain. As long as we accept pain as necessary to the human condition and turn to quick fixes for solutions, we will perpetuate it and will never create a new world order of unity in which we can live together in peace and prosperity.

Directing our power of will onto things other than God results in a much-talked-about state of mind that therapy has called "co-dependency." It is a learned behavior that is expressed through dependencies on people and things outside of ourselves for happiness, fulfillment, and self-definition. These dependencies, of course, do not bring about the desired result, but, rather, result in the neglect and diminishment of our true spiritual identity. The false self that emerges often expresses itself through compulsive habits, addictions, and other disorders which further increase alienation from our true identity. This creates a sense of shame, loss, fragmentation, and eventually hopelessness.

Codependency as a spiritual condition shadows the side of our nature that is unlimited love. We act out unequal relationships, and we give away our personal power, the power of our will, to outside influences. As we awaken and redirect our power of will Godward, we begin learning lessons of forgiveness and are reconnected to our true nature of unlimited love.

FORGIVENESS AND LOVE

The term *forgiveness* in Aramaic means "to untie and set free." It is a constant process. Whenever resentment and anger are at work toward an individual, a family, or a nation, we are bound to that individual or group by an emotional bond that appears indissoluble. Simply, the word *forgive* means "to give up all ill thoughts as well as outer contact until mediation can take place."

Love is not a feeling. Love is spiritual energy, pure creative energy at its highest level. Love expressed in human form actualizes your divine Self. Love is a divine energy that harmonizes and integrates, thus permitting our true divine identity to be expressed. One of the ways in which we direct our will Godward and open ourselves through divine love is through prayer. When we consciously hold the high watch for another, when we nurture feelings and beliefs of love, forgiveness, prosperity, health, and peace, when we consciously invite the inner Christ Spirit to express itself fully through our personality, we begin to redirect our will toward the good and create the increased potentiality of good for others.

The Berlin Wall came down because individuals (and, eventually, world leaders) directed their powers of will toward forgiveness and love. I believe that communism ended its reign in Russia because so many prayed for democracy. Although racism in America still exists, Dr. Martin Luther King's mission of nonviolent protest helped to change the consciousness of people all over the world, who are still singing as far away as Helsinki, Finland:

XII
—
144
—
XXI

> We shall overcome,
> We shall overcome,
> We shall overcome someday.
> If in our hearts we do believe,
> We shall overcome someday.

When we look today at national and international events, we hunger for acts of forgiveness on the part of world leaders. We still witness daily the horrors of war, homelessness, hunger and poverty, violence, teen pregnancies, addictions, discrimination and racism. We ask, "What happened to 'love thy neighbor as thyself'?" Jesus said: "Ye are the salt of the earth . . . . Ye are the light of the world. . . . Let your light so shine" (Mt. 5:13–16 KJV).

PRESSING SOCIAL ISSUES

When we choose to surrender, then the will of God expresses itself through our personal will. To surrender is to be willing to change. Old-world systems will have to be dissolved. The "Me" generation is over; the new millennium will mean global changes that affect everyone on the planet, changes from individual consciousness to global awareness, and a surrendering on a global scale of the personal will to the universal will of God.

We are the prodigal sons and daughters of this generation who have allowed our freedom of choice, our power of will, to fall prey to ignorance and misunderstanding of the divine law. Our lack of vigilance to the application of our powers of will in God-ward directions has created massive social problems over which we appear to have no control. As we explore the possibilities of how our individual and collective powers of will can redirect the social order in the new millennium, I'd like to share with you nine issues that I drew from the Atlanta Chapter of the League of Women Voters that are excellent examples of some of the most pressing issues we will face in the next century and in the new millennium:

1. The issue of crime has become enormous. Robbery, assault, rape, murder—events like these are becoming commonplace occurrences in our lives. Data suggests a shift in criminal activities from the cities to the suburbs for both the number and types of crimes that occur.

2. "Lost kids" or "at-risk kids"—"lost" not in the geographical sense, but "lost" in terms of direction (life goals and responsibilities), social skills, and general intellectual abilities. Examples of children who are lost in the system include the following: unwed teenage mothers, children who drop out of school for whatever reason, children who support or advocate violence as a way of resolution.

3. During recent congressional sessions, there has been ongoing debate over the stringency or leniency of environmental laws and regulations (for example, the Clean Water Act and the Endangered Species Act).

4. Social Security pays benefits to current retirees out of payroll taxes on current employers and workers. For now, revenues exceed expenditures, generating surpluses that are used to buy government bonds. But by about 2030, the system is expected to run deficits—leading to tax increases and benefit cuts. Some economists also say that the current system depresses the nation's already low savings rate.

5. According to a recent *New York Times* article, the federal budget deficit has fallen from 5 percent of the nation's total income in 1992 to 2.2 percent today. Yet, economists are arguing that unless the rate of growth of the outlays for Medicare and Medicaid are not cut back soon, the deficit will balloon, leading to tax increases and benefit cuts.

6. The single most frustrating factor for teachers is the intrusion of social problems into the classroom. Teachers, no matter how

XII

146

XXI

talented or dedicated, cannot combat poverty, child neglect and abuse, broken families, AIDS, drugs, homelessness, racism, and violence. Poor scholastic performance is a significant symptom of the social problems that affect our nation, and no amount of tinkering with the curriculum will cause schools to solve these problems on their own.

7. More than 1.6 million children came home to empty houses after school in 1991, nearly 8 percent of all grade-school children with working mothers, a Census Bureau study shows. More than 500,000 of these latchkey kids were under age twelve, the study said, including 23,000 six-year-olds, 45,000 seven-year-olds, and 47,000 eight-year-olds. The study also found that families spent about $21.8 billion on child care in 1991, paying an average of $63.30 a week. Families in poverty spent about 27 percent of their pretax income on child care, while other families spent about 7 percent of their pretax income.

8. *The Atlanta Journal Constitution* recently printed the following statistics:

• While women are 51.3 percent of the U.S. population, they account for 57.7 percent of the nation's poor.

• Between 1970 and 1990, 99 percent of the increase in poor families occurred among households headed by women. The phenomenon underscores the "feminization" of poverty.

• The increase in divorces and unmarried women with children has increased the feminization of poverty. Female-headed households accounted for 53.1 percent of poor families in 1991.

9. While the federal government continues to bicker over welfare dependency and runaway health-care costs, some thirty-eight states have taken charge of welfare overhaul.

These nine points of concern make us aware of the continuing breakdown in healthy social, political, and economic structures that are vital to global wholeness. Problems in education, economics, and family life are beyond critical points and have slid into chaos in many communities. Many schools have become war zones; homes have become hells, rather than havens; some economic systems diminish productivity and wealth, rather than expanding them; and political systems are vehicles of tyranny, rather than democracy. Conditions in these areas will take a dramatic turn for the better or the worse in the new millennium. The future that humankind creates will be determined by the direction in which we turn our individual and collective powers of will.

THE GROWTH OF INTERDEPENDENCE

The expanded global consciousness of the new millennium is racing to prevalence with the development of "instant communications" technologies such as the Internet. The world's ability to both capture and express its own diversity, simultaneously, is made real with the advent of fax machines, the five hundred-channel cable universe, and satellite TV. Life moves at a faster pace in the new millennium. As we move faster, we collide more frequently. Our interactions and our need for *interdependence* increase. No nation or group of nations can afford to operate in a vacuum. No person or organization of people can afford to ostracize another. In the new millennium, the contributions that each culture, and each individual of that culture, has to make will become more apparent. Interdependence is the key to a successful world economy.

The driving objective in the twenty-first century will be one of unfoldment, not exclusion. Required is a heightened sensitivity to the impact that one's own actions have on others in the interdependent society. The concepts of "oneness," "atonement," "one people," "one planet," and so on, will have to become the prime motivation in all political and economic decisions. None of these transitions will come to reality without a new established foundation of the unification of the will. In fact, it will become more important, indeed necessary, in the new millennium for humankind to move away from the concept of the activity of two separate "wills"—the personal will and the will of God—to an elevated understanding and awareness of God's will expressing itself as the personal will. This means ridding the race consciousness of the ideas of "separation from God." This "separation consciousness" has kept mankind in bondage to ego-serving wars, economic oppression and disparity, world hunger, strife, and poverty almost since the beginning of our history on the planet.

DISSOLVING THE SENSE OF SEPARATION

In *The Revealing Word*, Charles Fillmore says, "The will is the center in mind and body around which revolve all the activities that constitute consciousness. It is the avenue through which the I AM expresses its potentiality." This is a deeper understanding than many are willing to embrace now, even at the end of the twentieth century. "How can my stuff be the all-important will of God?" is the question that's most often asked by the new initiate to this way of thinking. But on a higher vibration, we know that, to ask this question is to deny our oneness with the Creator. It is to deny that God is all there is. In the new millennium, we must decide whether God is *all* or whether there is something else. The ancients tried to tell us this with the allegory of the Garden of Eden. Adam and Eve were admonished not to eat the fruit of the tree of the knowledge of good and evil. In other words, God told them not to think in terms of good and bad, of wrong and right, of should and shouldn't, and all of the other ego-driven, separation concepts that naturally follow as a result of seeing the One Life in such dualistic, schizophrenic ways. This can only lead to trouble and strife—the kind of trouble and strife that afflict our world in the present times.

As we move into the twenty-first century, the need for transforming the current consciousness of separateness is incumbent upon humankind. Crime, environmental degradation, issues confronting at-risk children, the precarious economy, the rising cost and unreliability of quality health care, and the decimating devastation of disease are just some of the plagues and pits along the pathway out of the twentieth century. But all of these result from the application of the "dual will" concept, that is, humanity turning our vision away from the true activity of God, or more aptly stated: humanity choosing to describe the omnipresent activity of God as something other than good. Perceptions of lack, attitudes of low self-worth, and feelings of powerlessness seduce our thoughts and feelings to repeatedly miss the mark. All of this must be transformed by us in the new millennium. Somewhere along the way, the focus will shift from "waiting for God to intervene," "waiting for Jesus to come," or "waiting for man to surrender his little will to the will of God," to an acceptance and knowing that there is only the activity of God operating in the universe, a seeing beyond deceptive appearances to the contrary, and a knowing that we are truly one with all things and that "all I give, I give to myself." Our conversation will change, reflecting our new willingness to accept responsibility for the world as we experience it. The whining and the "blaming" lingo that characterize the talk of the present decade will cease. The transformation comes when we fervently decree that "God is all there is— there is nothing else."

The transforming power of these thoughts actualized is immeasurable. World conditions will change when we change the basis for the decisions we make individually and collectively. Government leaders are an integral part of the changes that must be made to get us safely into the twenty-first century, but they are not the most critical element. It is the everyday, ordinary citizens of the world who will make the real difference. Despite decisions made by our governments and other power holders, it is up to each individual citizen to process the impact of those decisions properly so that our actions will, in turn, actualize from an awareness of the unified Will. We have to get to a place in our individual consciousness where we know that God is truly all there is and we direct our every activity so that it reflects the activity of God.

How does belief in One Will, One God, One Planet and People translate into a transformation of life in the new millennium? How are the aforementioned social sicknesses going to be healed through redirection of the will? How do growing poverty, increased dysfunction in families and the workplace, more broken homes, a failing economy, personal isolation and loneliness, and the continual destruction of our planet get reversed in the future? We must address these questions directly, lest our vision of peace and prosperity for all become just another "pie in the sky" alternative that denies worldly reality, rather than addressing it. No, our efforts at redirecting our power of will shall not occur in vain if we realize the profound strength of the individual and collective will and take responsibility for directing them Godward. Our wills must be used exclusively as vehicles of the higher Will. As we continually practice this, we will realize that the divine Will, the will of abundant good, is the only use of will which has any permanence or spiritual substance. Then we will be demonstrating the divine Will with every belief, choice, and activity, and we will have finally accepted "the kingdom prepared for us since the foundation of the world."

FIVE PRACTICAL WAYS

Here are five practical ways that we can begin to directly address the injustices, imbalances, and errors which we find abounding both within and all around us. Each of these ways refers to areas we must consider and work on as we seek to redirect our personal will in accordance with the divine Will:

1. *Seek personal truth.* We must engage in the reality of living beyond the ego to get in touch with our hearts. Intellect alone is not enough. We must allow the Spirit of God's will to work through our personal will. We must maintain our connection with God.

2. *Stay on course.* Positive change begins with the individual. We are on a greater mission that affects the lives of too many.

3. *Cultivate an awareness of our human resources.* A sense of shared humanity with people of all races, cultures, and ethnic backgrounds teaches us the value of each of us and the gifts we bring to the world order.

4. *Develop and maintain a sense of destiny.* Great leaders inspire others to the extent that they are willing to reach out into the future. Destiny becomes the magnet that pulls us to a sense of completion.

5. *Become involved in restructuring political, economic, social, and educational systems.* They must be workable in the new world. Management must flow from the inside out.

Diverse groups will work on these changes, and at some time there must be a "gathering" in which all spiritual traditions are acknowledged and actively share in this great plan for the new millennium. There are many individuals and groups who have worked in the past and are working right now to bring about multiple changes in favor of a new world order: Mother Teresa, Flying Doctors of America, Pavilion International, Boys and Girls Clubs, Dr. Johnnie Coleman, Barbara Marx Hubbard, Dr. Mary McCleod Bethune, Charles and Myrtle Fillmore, Dr. Joseph Murphy, and many, many others. As we raise our consciousness through the Godward direction of our powers of will, we find that we become pioneers in the movement of a new order in the new millennium.

As we practice these steps on our spiritual journey, we are not only expanding our own consciousness and enriching our own experience, we are also acting as a living example of faith and hope for others, who may have become discouraged. Remember that every effort you make in the direction of wholeness and the common good contributes to shifting the overall consciousness of our world.

As we continue our efforts to turn our individual and collective powers of will Godward, we will find that one day indeed "we shall overcome." We shall overcome the cloud of negative consciousness that covers much of our world now, a dark cloud made up of particles of hatred, resentment, anger, selfishness, and fear. If we could but see from a spiritual vantage point, we would see our future world radiantly alive with universal love, creativity, compassion, and diversity—people living together in wholeness and peace. As we enter the new millennium, we must let the divine Will be the "true north" on the inner compass we consult on this spiritual journey called "earth life" and we must remember that our personal power of will is the pointer on our compass. We may force it to temporarily point in another direction, but real nature is to return to true north, return to Good, return to God.

Dr. Barbara L. King is the founder and minister of the Hillside Chapel and Truth Center in Atlanta, Georgia. With a growing congregation of over five thousand, it has a visible and important role in the development of metropolitan Atlanta. She has been chairperson of Atlanta's Community Relations Commission and has many civic and community honors.

"Dr. Barbara," as she is affectionately called, has been awarded three honorary doctor of divinity degrees as well as a master of social work degree from Atlanta University. She has just completed course work for a doctorate in educational administration.

The founder-president of the Barbara King School of Ministry, Barbara has been vice-president of the International New Thought Alliance. Her extensive travel and universal appeal helped the Hillside Chapel to be the first African-American New Thought affiliate to establish a sister church in South Africa.

Barbara King is the author of numerous books, including the following: *Transform Your Life; How to Have a Flood and Not Drown;* and *Love Your Body Temple.*

XII

154

XXI

CHAPTER IX

THE POWER OF LIFE

Life is the one power that seems easy to understand, and that may be the reason why we often do not understand it very deeply. Life is a natural expression of our being, and it is what gives expression to all the powers. Without life, the other powers cannot express themselves in this earthly realm.

So life needs the other powers, and the other powers need life. Life is the animating, acting principle that activates the pure spiritual essence, the substance, and shapes it through our thoughts, words, and actions. However, by itself, life is not truly intelligent; it needs directive power from the other eleven faculties. With faith, life perceives; with imagination, life conceives; with will, life chooses, and so on.

Interestingly, it is Judas who represents life. Judas, the money carrier, betrays Jesus out of a misguided plan to force Jesus to reveal himself. Don't be too quick to condemn Judas, however, for he is like you and me. Don't we often bring our spiritual ideals down to earth in order to justify our habits and expectations? Don't we betray our highest visions in order to meet our mundane obligations? This is life, ignorant of its highest calling, misappropriating its power.

Life is the power of acquisition, appropriation, and desire. Like will, it has a legitimate role but finds itself in trouble unless it surrenders entirely to its highest calling. After Judas hangs himself in shame, the disciple who replaces him is named Mathias, the equivalent to Matthew. Like Matthew, who is will, Mathias symbolizes the lifting up of the life faculty in total surrender to the divine Will. Life, surrendered to God, attains everything.

Toward Living the
Abundant Life

Joan Gattuso

Isat in prayer this morning at the bedside of a precious, kind, loving woman, who was sleeping soundly on the first morning after surgery for cervical cancer. She is a student of metaphysics, an active Unity member for a number of years, a woman who studies, prays, and meditates daily.

She was struck with terror two weeks previously when, without any prior indication as to her physical diagnosis, her primary care physician had sent her to another doctor, who proposed several possible dates for surgery. Dumbfounded, she asked, "Why in heaven's name do I need surgery?"

The doctor replied, "Didn't your primary care physician tell you why you were coming to see me?"

He had not. The doctor gave her the startling news of the cervical cancer.

We who are free of disease and without such shocking news can believe we understand what such a diagnosis must mean to a person. We believe we are able to be empathetic and feel what the patient feels. I have personally and deeply learned that this assumption just isn't so.

For over a dozen years I had sat with, prayed with, done healing work with, meditated with, and worked on various other levels with cancer patients. I had tremendous faith in their abilities to be

157

healed or, at the very least, to have their disease arrested. I thought I had a degree of understanding as to what individuals in my congregation were experiencing, what they were feeling, what emotions and fears were surging through their consciousness when receiving such a diagnosis. My understanding was naive.

Then one day in August 1991, a new physician I had visited called with some test results. I knew everything was all right. I had been a metaphysician since my early twenties. Several years later I had committed my life to God and entered ministerial school. I had meditated and prayed every day for over twenty years. I practiced forgiveness instantly whenever experiencing even the slightest upset. I had been a non-meat eater and natural foods advocate for most of my life. That day, however, I received the most devastating news of my life. I had cancer cells in the lining of my uterus.

I went numb. My head was spinning. I instantly broke out in a cold sweat. The news was so devastating that my consciousness began to leap out of my body. The doctor continued talking, but I was no longer listening, could no longer hear. My mind began to race.

How could this be? I felt as if I had failed and failed miserably as a Truth student, let alone as a teacher and minister. My being was somehow wired that, if one does everything "right"—right consciousness, right prayer life, right meditation, right dietary practices, right exercise, right thought, right loving heart, right feelings—then one is invincible, or nearly so.

Having been a Truth student for so many years, I did not rush to look up cancer in Louise Hays' *You Can Heal Your Life* or in my old copy of *Divine Remedies*. I already knew the mind-body connection. I knew that a pervasive thought consistently held in mind creates a corresponding condition within the body.

Well, if I had harbored deep hurt, longstanding resentments, or carried hatred, they clearly did not live on any conscious level. Nor did it appear that I had "rejected my femininity."

So often we can use such teachings as a magic formula to explain away any unpleasant situation. I know I certainly had done so in the past. Right arm injured? Oh, that means the masculine part of you is afraid to move forward, to extend yourself. Hurt your left knee? That must mean that your female aspect needs to exercise humility. Heart problem? That's "blocked" love. And on and on we can go.

I wrestled with this startling information through the night like Jacob at Jabbock Ford and would not let the "angel" go until there was an exchange of blessings. There ended up being many blessings with this experience, none of which could have been seen when I was looking through lenses of terror.

Illness as a Gift

I remember being on the telephone with Silent Unity, sobbing my story to a prayer worker of remarkable tenderness and compassion, who affirmed over and over that I was not a failure as a Truth student and a minister because of my diagnosis. She said that this was a soul lesson for me, but not just for me. It was a lesson for all those I was then serving and for all those I would serve in the future. It was and would be a blessing for me and countless others. Although I was unable to take in all that she was saying, her words nonetheless calmed me and resonated as "Truth" within me.

Subsequently I spent a period of time with a friend, Dennis Adams, who is internationally recognized as a healer. He told me, "This cancer is a gift. This is *your* gift."

I scoffed and replied, "If this were a gift, I would prefer that it come in one of those beautiful little turquoise blue Tiffany boxes."

His eyes pierced through me. He took both my hands and once again declared with increased volume, "This is a gift!" His voice lowered somewhat and he added, "You don't see it now, but you will."

He was right.

My experience did not usher in my demise, but, rather, it got me to step aside and re-evaluate every aspect of my life. It forced me to look at those little things in life that can seem to be so important, so valuable, but are truly valueless. Swiftly, I began to peel all the inconsequential stuff, all the littleness, away.

Life and its spiritual wonder became of utmost significance. My personal expression of that divine life force became of tantamount importance. I immediately ceased doing any of the "shoulds" and "oughts" that had consumed so much of my time. I learned that what was really crucial for me was to keep my tanks on full and to give to myself, rather than *always* choosing to give of myself to others. I had given previously to such an extent that there was very little of me left for myself. This is not an uncommon situation for a minister or a caregiver.

My friend Dennis was right. It was a gift. It just did not look like any other gift I had been given. This gift caused me to go deeper within my own soul and into the heart of God than I had ever traveled in my twenty-plus years of meditation and prayer.

Three weeks after major surgery, barely able to walk erectly, I traveled to New York City to study for eight days with His Holiness, the Dalai Lama. Why? Because I knew I had to go. My husband David recalls he questioned his sanity when he put me on the plane, but he also trusted the healing process. And if my going to be with the Dalai Lama was part of that healing process, then he, too, knew I must go.

I received two huge gifts during those eight days. First, the Dalai Lama mentioned that there are times when, due to an illness, one may have to offer up certain body parts. If that is required and it is done with right-mindedness, then the experience can lead the individual into greater spiritual depths. This wisdom brought me peace and greater understanding.

Second, several days later he was asked by one of the 4000 in attendance how much time he recommended we (not the 150 lamas present, but the rest of the Westerners present) spend each day in meditation. The Dalai Lama paused, reflected, and then stated, "Four hours." The collective gasp of those 4000 reverberated throughout Madison Square Garden.

Prior to that declaration, I thought I was doing pretty darn well by meditating forty-five minutes a day. Four hours was not realistic for me, given my heavy schedule, but at that moment I made the commitment to begin meditating two hours a day. Now, there are many who may say meditating for so long is unnecessary, and for them it may be. For me such a high level of commitment to my meditative life has caused astonishing and remarkable openings in consciousness and in the outer picture of my life.

There is no mistaking it. There is an enormous difference between being in a deep, meditative state for between twenty and forty-five minutes once or twice a day and going into that inner chamber which Jesus spoke about for two hours each day. I committed myself to the new meditative regimen.

I began to heal very quickly, so much so that when I went for my next postoperative examination, the surgeon was flabbergasted at the degree of healing and the look of the tissue. I told him it was due to meditation and working with healing light. He raised his eyebrows. When he remarked that the pain which I was experiencing from the adhesions would never completely go away, I disagreed and told him that I was not willing to "learn to live with it," and that it *would* go away.

It did.

Life Is a Precious Gift

Ancient Eastern scriptures speak of the life force being like a coiled serpent seated at the base of the spine, a tremendous source of energy and power lying in wait, ready to respond to the com-

XII

161

XXI

mand from the individual, through meditation or the spoken word, to rise up and bring forth a new level of aliveness.

I called upon the coiled life force to rise up and move out and renew and restore every cell and function of my body. Every cell responded. Once, while attending a Deepak Chopra presentation, I heard him speak of our ability to have "happy cells" when we are in a state of optimum health. My cells had become *very* happy!

What is life? Well, it is a spiritual power. We know that. But it is so much more. Life is the most precious gift of God. It wasn't until I feared my individual expression of life would be over decades and decades too soon that I could begin to fathom its depth of meaning. And it wasn't my fear that did it. The fear simply was a catalyst that caused me to work to release it to the Holy Spirit and move deeper into the heart of God. My own heart was filled with an unfathomable gratitude to be alive, to have been given the "unnecessary medical test," to have the cancer cells discovered at the earliest stage, to be given a clean bill of health, to have my life back and have it back different from before.

We dissipate our life force, not by sexual activity as many early metaphysicians taught, but by being all too often consumed by the littleness of life. When we do so we miss out on the magnificence of life that is possible.

USELESS AND UNNECESSARY SUFFERING

Consider how much of your life is given over to that which robs your spirit of its vitality—from involvement in a career which does not bring joy, to friends and family who dominate your spare time without supporting you in consciousness, to obligations and demands and expectations and the drive to attempt always to please others.

Oh, we may say: "Sure, I'll do it," or "Wrong? Nothing's wrong here," or "I'll be okay." But we don't want to do it. There is something wrong. Things are definitely not "okay." If we remain disconnected from our own desires and worth long enough, we become so far removed from our core that we no longer know we aren't okay. Sometimes it does take the proverbial, cosmic two-by-four to wake us up, so we begin to value only that which is valuable and let all the rest go.

"Todd" is endearing, kind, generous, and remarkably successful in the business world. He is equally remarkably insecure. He lives each day of his life in total fear and anxiety that, at any given moment, he may lose his high-ranking position with an international corporation, where his annual salary is in the middle six-figure range.

Todd literally earns ten times more than his contemporaries and feels very undeserving of his financial success. Todd lives in an inner world of constant turmoil, anxiety, and perpetual worry—worry that at any moment his career will be snatched away. This is clearly what the great Unity teacher Ed Rabel always called "useless and unnecessary suffering." It is useless and unnecessary because Todd is no ordinary guy. Todd, to anyone else's yardstick, is extraordinary. The problem is that Todd is far removed from seeing himself as extraordinary. He barely sees himself as ordinary. He believes he is an "impostor" for having the career, living the life, having the responsibilities, having the family he does not believe he deserves.

The bottom line is, says Todd: "I am not happy. I'm tied up in knots. I worry all day that the CEO will wake up and realize he has made a big mistake in retaining me. I'm making myself sick, and I'm so unhappy."

Todd is literally dissipating not only his energy, but his very life force. He is depleted emotionally and spiritually.

Perhaps you or one you love has been in a similar circumstance. All of your energy is directed into the outer aspects of life. For Todd it was career. For others it can be seeking approval, giving to others to such an extent that there is nothing left, or running so fast that there is never time to stop and reflect.

XII

163

XXI

All such paths rob us of our aliveness. When living from such a plane, life begins to become increasingly meaningless. The joy is gone. The vitality is nowhere to be found. Life is, at best, just the day-by-day motions you force yourself through.

AFFIRMATIONS FOR A HAPPY LIFE

If you are living such a life, begin right now, gently but firmly, to speak to your innermost being and communicate the following:

This need not be. I need not live my life attempting always to please others. I need not live in such an unhappy state. I need not suffer.

Once the communication has begun and you begin to truly realize that the states which are depleting your very life energy need not be, it is very effective to affirm:

I (first name) *am now learning to live my life.*
I (first name) *now experience living my own life fully.*
I (first name) *am now truthful with myself about my feelings.*
I (first name) *now choose to live from a state of joy instead of pain.*

The most effective way I have found to use affirmations is to set aside twenty to thirty minutes, take a notebook, and write out the affirmation, being certain to insert your first name. It can be one of the above or one you create, but it must be written in the present tense and be very positive.

Initially, it doesn't even matter if you believe the affirmation to be true or not. What matters is that it is spiritually true. After each writing of the affirmation, immediately write the first thoughts that come to mind. If you have been giving yourself away to others to such an extent that there is no "you" left for yourself, when you first write this affirmation: *I, Todd, deserve to experience joy in living my life fully now,* your inner voice is not going to say, "Yes, Todd, you're absolutely right." Rather, your response will be something like a sarcastic, "Oh, yeah, right!"

Then, I, Todd, *deserve to experience joy in living my life fully now.*
A probable response: "I have no life."
Then, I, Todd, *deserve to experience joy in living my life fully now.*
A probable response: "I don't even know what joy is."
Then, I, Todd, *deserve to experience joy in living my life fully now.*
A probable response: "I don't even know what my life is."

As you continue for several days, those negative responses will begin to become less and less negative. What you are doing is releasing much of the dammed-up energy that has been robbing you of your vitality.

In your writing, when you come to the point where you agree with and say "Yes," to the affirmation, then you will no longer need to write the negative responses. For there won't be any left. At this point write the affirmation from ten to twenty times a day for several days, and then move on to a new affirmation.

This really works and moves the healing process right along.

In your own life begin to re-evaluate how you spend your days, weeks, months, years. Are you engaged in a career that brings joy and abundance? If not, your life force is being strangled. Are you expressing your deepest emotions, and do you value your feelings? If not, your life force is being strangled. Are you comfortable with your body, and can you achieve sexual expression that fills you with bliss? If not, your life force is being strangled.

The Metaphysical View—A Piece of the Puzzle

So what do we as metaphysicians do with our metaphysical view of life when we personally face, or one dear to us faces, a life-threatening disease? It is important that we not throw the baby out with the bath water.

We can honestly explore the thought-body connection in the affliction. But when we do so, we must not get so hung up that this simplistic explanation is all that we can see. It may indeed be a tremendous insight as to where we individually need to be doing our healing and forgiveness work, but it is a *piece* of the puzzle and not the whole puzzle.

Once, I worked with a young man who had a number of minor but irritating physical problems. The medical doctors were unable to pinpoint the cause of any one of the conditions, and they all seemed unrelated.

"Terry" visited specialist after specialist—with no permanent relief. He would have a recurring and irritating rash, metaphysically explained away as irritation over delays and as a babyish way to get attention; a sudden and unexplained fever, explained as anger; acute muscle aches followed by waves of weakness, explained as a longing to be loved and held. There were other symptoms, as well.

What happened in the medical arena was that one physician had another young patient with very similar symptoms. She began her own inquiry into Terry's and the other young man's medical histories. She came up with nothing. She then brought the two young men together. To their astonishment, they discovered they had been raised in the same ethnic neighborhood of a large industrial city and as children they had lived only two blocks apart. Further investigation revealed that they had spent countless hours playing in a large empty lot owned by a steel mill.

Over the next several years several more young people came forward with similar symptoms—all having been raised within blocks of one another. The common denominator shared by all was playing in the same empty lot, a lot in which several years before a huge amount of industrial waste had been dumped. This lot served as a playground, since there was no community center or school playground nearby. This highly toxic piece of earth had literally polluted their young bodies and left contaminants that would not present themselves until years later. Eventually the company was sued, and the class-action suit was settled out of court.

The sole reason Terry had rashes, fevers, and muscle problems was not because he was babyish, angry, looking for love and attention, or afraid to move forward in his life. It was because as a child he had spent month after month in a toxic playground. There is always more to the story, sometimes a lot more. The reason why cannot always be so easily categorized and placed in a tidy little metaphysical box.

Live the Life You Are Meant to Live

Good and healing and blessings can come out of any condition, even from what we view as the most dreadful, if we would but open ourselves to that larger good and fuller healing. The AIDS virus, as dreadful as it is, has brought so many of those afflicted and their loved ones, friends, and families—in many cases—to a much deeper place of honesty, communication, tenderness, compassion, and love.

I believe that, as we work with the life force and have a sincere desire to individuate this power to a greater degree, it is important we truly not judge—not judge ourselves, not judge the condition, not judge another.

Nonjudgment is certainly not always easy, but it is always necessary. When we do judge, we block the possibility of all that could be. To judge a condition never assists in healing that condition. In many instances a condition is present to open our hearts, to crack open our shells of protection.

It wasn't until I thought I might no longer have my life that I truly began to live my life. Rather than living what should have been my life, my focus had always been others—the congregation, the church, my family responsibilities. When I thought I would no longer know life as "Joan," all the other priorities quickly shifted in their importance. Living life according to others' expectations was no longer important or even a consideration. It took such a shock to truly start living the life I was meant to live.

RISING OUT OF RACE CONSCIOUSNESS

I realize I live in a pretty rarified world, a world where people do not need to be reminded to be PC (politically correct). In my world those within it seek to live life as conscious beings every moment of every day. Endeavoring to have their every action be mindful, non-judgmental, kind, compassionate, and loving, this is exactly the kind of world they experience.

I see such conscious beings moving into the next millennium building a bridge that will provide an access for countless others to cross over, leaving behind the judgments and fears which have separated our human family in the past.

Since the first recorded history, we have been engaged in slowly ascending the spiral from one stage of realization, becoming familiar and comfortable there, to the next stage, which is awakening us to climb higher. There we adjust and become comfortable, before the call is heard once again and race consciousness makes its next quantum advancement. Now, too, we can hear the call if we will but listen and follow the Spirit into experiencing more wholeness and holiness.

In order to heal and dissolve the walls that have separated us, it is crucial that we look at these barriers and honestly ask: "Does this serve me? Does this serve the world? Does it serve me to hate my brother-in-law because he is of a different religion than our family's? Does it serve the world for me to treat someone as an unequal because of his or her being a different race from mine?"

If we are mindful, our answers are an emphatic, "No! Of course not!"

All attitudes and states of mind that separate us on any level from one another—be it racial, ethnic, sexual, or gender—are based entirely on fear. Fear binds us and keeps us and our thoughts locked in a tight, narrow, suffocating little box. It was out of fear that Cain fought with Abel. It was out of fear that the fractured groups of today fight with each other.

It is fear that must be addressed and healed in order to cross that bridge hand in hand into the next millennium. In order to do this it is necessary to stop seeing anyone an enemy and start being able to see all as individuals doing their best, "just like me."

This is one of my favorite techniques for conscious living. I learned it several years back in my initial exploration into Tibetan Buddhism. It is so practical, helpful, and true. Here it is in all its simplicity. Whenever you judge anyone or anything, right after you think it or say it, add to your judgment . . . "just like me."

Here are some examples:

"He's such a thoughtless person . . . just like me."

"She's always so critical . . . just like me."

"What an awful, rude driver . . . just like me."

"What a kind, loving person . . . just like me."

"They are such generous souls . . . just like me."

Get the idea? It really works. Soon you will notice your judgments and separating thoughts begin to decrease, and you will no longer view others as enemies, but as advancing souls, "just like me."

Underneath our familial heritage, underneath our gender, underneath our race, underneath our sexual preferences, we are all the same. We all share the oneness, the allness that is God. Underneath our various veneers, we are one. When we are healed of our petty thoughts, prejudices, and attitudes, we can finally realize this wondrous Truth of our being.

In the millennium that lies before us like a clean slate, I see more and more of us arising and walking across the bridge, embracing our divinity, and realizing the great spiritual Truth that we are all equally God's beloved sons and daughters.

Holy Sexuality

When I first came into Unity one of my early teachers taught that, in order to fully access the life force, we must sublimate all sexual energy and do away with all desire. The way we were to do this was by meditating on blue or purple and drawing the energy up from the second *chakra* into the crown *chakra* and out the top of the head. I'd try and all I'd get were headaches! Then I decided that perhaps my teacher was missing the point.

In my book *A Course in Love,* I wrote a chapter entitled "Holy Sex." This has shocked some people. I heard comments like: "I can't believe Joan had the courage to write about sex being sacred and holy," and "She actually wrote about *that!*"

The implications of such statements are that all metaphysical types are asexual beings. I have noticed quite the opposite to be the case. When we awaken ourselves spiritually, that awakening quickens the flow of the divine in all of our power centers, including the center of life itself. This is not something to be repressed or ashamed of or ignored or considered dirty or unspiritual. Rather, it is one part of our spiritual nature, a part that can give us much pleasure and lead us into a holy union with our partner. Sexual expression at its highest level is an expression of our fully awakened spirituality. It is not separate and apart from, but a part *of* our spiritual Self.

In the holy expression of sexual energy, each partner has learned to isolate the pure sexual energy and direct this energy from the second chakra up the spinal column and into the heart. Once this is attained, the couple is now prepared to move their lovemaking into an entirely new dimension.

Here is a wonderful technique to assist you in learning how to move this energy. While you and your partner are sharing an intimate embrace, begin to breathe in sync, one with the other. Then you both begin to move the focus of your energy from the sexual center into the heart center. The ability to do this for some comes quite easily, and for others it will take practice. As the energy moves into the heart during lovemaking, the experience shared by the two of you will begin to intensify and magnify.

It is at times like these that we can actually experience the sacred within our physical unions. Rather than viewing the sexual as the basest part of our nature, I believe we must honor it as a vital part of who we are. To deny this is to cut ourselves off from the very root of our life force.

What Lies Ahead

What lies ahead for us and the generations to follow, as we move into the next millennium? At the very thought of what is possible, I am filled with awe.

I look at the little children of today and see young, even tiny, bodies that are now housing great souls. Many of the little ones I encounter are awake, advanced souls. It is our responsibility to be equally as clear, in order to access the very core of life and live from its center, so that we can consciously and effectively support the ongoing spiral as we all move together into the possibility of what could be.

As each one comes to value self and align with the spiritual expression of the life force, we add to the collective energy of life, a pure vibration. Within this vibration is the seeding of a transformed world.

Do I think this will happen in an instant? Not in one instant, but rather in that instant being joined to the next blessed instant, connecting with the next and the next. As these divine moments continue to expand, we shall experience not just an instant of love, not just a moment of peace, not just a glimpse of our aliveness, but longer and longer expanses of time in which we shall have a collective experience of love, peace, and aliveness.

This dynamic expansion of the possibility becoming our reality has already begun. I know many who experience life in such a glorious manner. I do so myself more and more.

To me this is living the more abundant life that Jesus spoke of 2000 years ago. Isn't it time we start living it now and even more fully into the future?

Joan Gattuso was ordained a Unity minister in 1979. A graduate of Miami University in Ohio, Joan has emerged as a leader, teacher, and counselor to the New Thought and New Age community. She is the founding minister of Unity of Greater Cleveland in Cleveland, Ohio.

A frequent contributor to *Science of Mind* and *Unity Magazine*, Joan is the author of the best-selling book: *A Course in Love*. Her new book is *A Course in Life*.

Rev. Gattuso is a student of Tibetan Buddhism and has studied extensively with His Holiness, the Dalai Lama. She is also a long-time student and teacher of *A Course in Miracles*.

Chapter X

The Power of Power

Without contemplation, the power of power, like life, is subtle enough for us to easily miss its meaning. At first glance, power is the equivalent of strength, and in the popular mind, they are understood that way. Yet true power has more in common with will.

Power, according to Charles Fillmore, is our innate control over our thoughts and feelings. This would link power to faith, the perceiving power, yet power itself is the distinct ability to choose whether we stay with a perception or allow that thought to enter the gateway of our consciousness.

In metaphysical Christianity and New Thought, the power of the word—whether thought or spoken—is considered the basis for all cocreation with God. So the power to choose our thoughts, to will our thoughts and feelings, is absolutely vital. It is how we choose our own reality and it is how we choose, finally, to become completely whole and one with the Christ.

Philip is the disciple who represents power. The name *Philip* means "lover of horses," which, metaphysically, means "the master of the vital forces." For power to become master, however, it needs the power of will and, like will, the other powers as well, particularly wisdom, love, and understanding.

Power Shift: A New Paradigm for the New Millennium

Robert Brumet

P*ower!* What image does that word evoke for you? For me, a variety of images come to mind—mostly images of nature. As a child, I would watch the summer thunderstorms roll across the midwestern plains. I was awestruck by the presence of the breathtaking power that danced before my eyes and thundered in my ears. As a young adult, I visited Niagara Falls for the first time. Standing only a few yards from this colossal waterfall, I could feel the earth vibrating beneath my feet and I could feel the electric charge in the air tingling my skin. I was nearly mesmerized by the roar of more than a million gallons of water a second cascading into an enormous gorge 165 feet below. Many years later, I saw evidence of the potentially destructive power of nature when I visited a neighborhood that had just been ravaged by a tornado. I stared incredulously at the display of leveled homes, overturned vehicles, and uprooted trees. I saw something that I wouldn't believe if I hadn't seen it myself: about a dozen stalks of straw imbedded in a tree trunk as if someone had fired them from a gun! Nature has presented me with some vivid images of her stunning power.

Not everyone would associate images of nature with the word *power*. You might have different associations with this word, depending upon your personal history. A military person sees images of massive armies and powerful weapons. A historian recalls a powerful historical figure or a mighty civilization from the past. A business person imagines controlling a vast business enterprise involving thousands of people and many millions of dollars. The word *power* may mean many different things to many different people.

NEGATIVE USES OF POWER

To some people the word *power* may conjure up negative or painful feelings. Many of us have memories of being hurt by someone who had power over us. Perhaps the injury was not even intentional, yet the memories are still painful. Oppressive political or economic systems have hurt many people. Religious institutions and religious leaders have been perpetrators of the misuse of power. Some of us were hurt by our own parents. Many of us have been victimized by the abuse of power.

All too often we hear about negative uses of power. History is replete with stories of individuals, institutions, and nations tyrannizing the populace. Hitler, Stalin, Mao Tse-tung, Napoleon, Julius Caesar, and Genghis Khan are just a few examples of individuals whose use of power has caused great suffering for many people.

As a child growing up in the forties, I recall, as some of my earliest memories, seeing photos of the mushroom cloud formed by the atom bombs dropped on Hiroshima and Nagasaki. I also remember seeing photographs and news clips of the horrors of Nazi concentration camps. Although I was too young to comprehend the meaning of these images, they were nonetheless burned deep into my psyche. I did not understand why people did such things to one another. Fifty years later, I still do not understand.

Humankind's misuse of power has caused great suffering. The continued abuse of power threatens the end of human life—and perhaps *all* life—on this planet. Not only humans, but nearly all living species on our planet, have suffered from our abuse of power. This shortsightedness has caused the extinction of many species of plants and animals and has seriously disrupted the ecology of the earth itself. Our use of power must undergo a radical shift if we are to survive the next millennium.

CRISIS PRECEDES TRANSFORMATION

This radical shift is not only necessary for our survival but may also be an evolutionary imperative—a necessary step in the development of our species. Throughout the history of life on this planet (including human history), we see an important principle at work: A crisis always precedes a transformation. Barbara Marx Hubbard writes in *The Evolutionary Journey*:

> Crises precede transformation. Before every quantum change, "problems" emerge—limits to growth, stagnation, unmanageable complexity, impending catastrophes, disintegration. From the perspective of the present, the crises look like mistakes, deadly errors in the system. But from the perspective after the quantum transformation, these problems are seen to be "evolutionary drivers," vital stimulants which trigger astounding "design innovations."[1]

At the time of the crisis we are usually enmeshed in the belief that "something is wrong!" Only with the perspective of time—often many years—do we see the crisis in a different context: a birthing of something radically new.

Pierre Teilhard de Chardin was another visionary who saw our present crisis as part of an evolutionary imperative. A Jesuit priest and a renowned paleontologist, Teilhard formulated a view of the physical universe as a dynamic manifestation of ever-evolving consciousness. In this system, humanity—as a species—is an essential link in the progressive unfoldment of consciousness from the most primal substance of the universe to the culmination of all evolution, which Teilhard referred to as the Omega point—conscious oneness with God.

Evolution, according to Teilhard, occurs in stages. The development of consciousness occurs within each stage according to a pattern of increasing complexity. When a certain threshold of complexity is reached, a convergence takes place—a critical point at which evolution can make a quantum leap into an entirely new level of consciousness. Teilhard recognized the period immediately before the quantum leap as being very critical—a time of great crisis.

In the Chinese language, the word for *crisis* is formed by a combination of two other words: one meaning "danger," the other, "opportunity." The Chinese long ago recognized a crisis as "a dangerous opportunity." The English word *crisis* is derived from a Greek word meaning "to decide." And one of the dictionary definitions of *crisis* is "a crucial turning point." Indeed, we *are* at a point of decision, a turning point, a crisis.

So the bad news may be good news after all! Our corruption of power may simply be a sign of our evolutionary immaturity. Our awareness of the grave danger facing us may be a sign that it is time for us, as a species, to grow up. As children, we could perhaps afford to be self-centered and shortsighted; as adults we cannot, for we may finally be seeing that continued immaturity may lead to self-destruction.

To avoid self-destruction, we must learn to use our power wisely. To help us envision the right use of power in the next century and the next millennium, let us briefly look back at the past millennium and examine the ways in which we experienced our power at that stage of our evolution.

The Last Millennium

In the tenth century C.E. most of Europe was dominated by the Christian church. The vast majority of individuals lived with very little sense of personal power. For the average man, it would seem that the king owned his body and the church owned his soul. His life and fate were determined almost completely by the land barons, the aristocracy, and the Church hierarchy. Women and children had even less power, for they were considered little more than the property of their husbands or fathers. Most people's belief systems and senses of values were dictated almost exclusively by the Church and its officials. Humankind's relationship with God was that of a helpless child at the mercy of an omnipotent—and often angry— God. Virtually all power—spiritual, political, and economic—was highly concentrated within the hands of a few elite individuals. It would appear that the average person felt quite powerless—a victim of the world and the universe in which he or she lived.

About five centuries later—approximately halfway through the last millennium—a radical shift began to occur. A rebirth, a renaissance, began to take place within the Western world. The Reformation would soon occur within the Christian church. The Scientific Revolution was about to emerge. An age of Enlightenment would follow. Suddenly, it would seem, humankind was beginning to find a new vision of itself and a new sense of its own power. No longer a victim of forces beyond its control, no longer in servitude to political or spiritual overlords, humanity began to awaken to its power of reason.

"I think, therefore I am."

These words, written by the French mathematician-philosopher René Descartes, underscore the emphasis on the power of reason and inquiry, not simply revelation, as a source of truth. God began to take a backseat to reason. With each passing century God's importance in human life would seem to shrink to near nothingness.

Perhaps the young and brilliant Pico della Mirandola best summed up the new spirit of optimism and the new vision of humanity's potential. The following words, spoken in C.E. 1486 by the 23-year-old scholar, reflect this new vision of the creation of humankind and of its place in the universe. These words are spoken as if the gods were speaking to a newly created humanity:

> Neither an established place, nor a form belonging to you alone, nor any special function have We given to you, O Adam, and for this reason, that you may have and possess, according to your desire and judgment, whatever place, whatever form, and whatever functions you shall desire. The nature of other creatures, which has been determined, is confined within the bounds prescribed by Us. You, who are confined by no limits, shall determine for yourself your own nature, in accordance with your own free will, in whose hand I have placed you.[2]

Within three decades after Pico's oration, Columbus would discover the New World, Copernicus would make the first astronomical observation and outline his heliocentric theory of the solar system, Leonardo da Vinci would paint *The Last Supper*, Erasmus would translate the New Testament into Latin, Michelangelo would complete his famous painting in the Sistine chapel, and Martin Luther would post his ninety-five theses on the church door at Wittenberg, thus beginning the Protestant Reformation.

FROM VICTIM TO VICTOR

Clearly, Western humanity was throwing off the shackles of victim consciousness and declaring itself—through the power of reason and scientific inquiry—a victor over the forces of nature and the

XII

179

XXI

circumstances of its birth. This attitude of *victor* has remained with us for the last five hundred years. Moving from *victim* to *victor* seemingly has served us well. One simply has to look at the progress we have made in the last five centuries. We have created a mighty civilization that rests largely upon the foundation of science and reason and upon the attitude that we are to be *victors,* not victims of life.

With this new identity of *victor* we have used our power to effect changes in our environment and in our lifestyle. Through the power of technology, we have radically altered the world around us and we have changed the life of virtually every human being on earth. Through the power of the written and the spoken word, we have influenced the minds and the hearts of countless numbers of people. Through political and military power, we have altered the lives of millions of people—sometimes in rather horrific ways.

We have become extremely adept at understanding and changing the world around us but have been woefully inept at understanding and changing ourselves. We have mastered nature and mastered nations but have failed miserably at mastering ourselves. Albert Einstein once observed, "The unleashed power of the atom has changed everything save our modes of thinking, and we thus drift toward unparalleled catastrophes."[3] We have unleashed the forces of nature but remain ignorant of our own nature. It's not just the power of the atom bomb which threatens us, but it is our ignorance of ourselves which puts us in real danger. Until we place as much value on understanding and controlling ourselves as we have placed on understanding and controlling the world around us, we will continue to inflict suffering on all living creatures.

As we approach the beginning of a new millennium, we can see the limitations of the "victor" viewpoint. We have conquered nature at the price of alienating ourselves from it. We have conquered land, sea, air, and space at the price of alienating ourselves from one another. We have reasoned our way into self-alienation. We have conquered everything except ourselves.

XII

180

XXI

Until we learn to control ourselves, we cannot safely control the forces of nature. Until we have gained self-knowledge, we will never truly understand nature. The greatest power we have is the power to understand and to control ourselves.

This is not a new thought. Spiritual teachers have taught this for many centuries. More than twenty-five hundred years ago, Gautama Buddha spoke these words to his disciples:

> If one man conquers in battle a thousand times a thousand men, and if another conquers himself, he is the greatest of conquerors. One's own self conquered is better than all other people conquered; not even a god could change into defeat the victory of a man who has vanquished himself.[4]

How does one conquer "one's own self"? The Buddha developed an elaborate system of instruction that answers this very question. The heart of his teaching is this: The cause of suffering is egocentric desire, and the overcoming of suffering lies in recognizing and dissolving egocentric desire. Five hundred years after the time of the Buddha, Jesus of Nazareth spoke these words: "He who finds his life will lose it, and he who loses his life for my sake will find it" (Mt. 10:39 RSV). Jesus embodied this very teaching in his own life. He told his disciples: "The words that I say to you I do not speak on my own authority; but the Father who dwells in me does his works" (Jn. 14:10 RSV). About twenty-five years later, the apostle Paul wrote these words: "I have been crucified with Christ; it is no longer I who live, but Christ who lives in me" (Gal. 2:20 RSV). All great spiritual teachers and teachings have told us of the need to let go of our ego-centered way of life.

Until we do this we will never create a truly new world. Until we are willing to surrender the personal self to a Higher Power, we will continue to re-create different versions of the old world. Yet, the old world that we have created is not a bad world. What we have done is right, perhaps perfect, for what needed to be done. Like adolescents, we have flexed our muscles and experienced our sense of independence. Now it is time for us to become spiritual adults; it is time for us to create a new world.

From Victor to Vehicle

Having moved from *victim* to *victor*, it is time for us to become *vehicles* for the divine Will. As vehicles for divine Will, we see ourselves as instruments operating on behalf of a Higher Power. Still, this instrument, this vehicle, is far from passive or powerless. We, as agents of the divine, have no limits to our power. And we, disconnected from the divine, have no power whatsoever; in truth, no existence whatsoever.

As *vehicles*, we acknowledge the omnipotence of God and the supremacy of God's will, as did our medieval brothers and sisters. At the same time we can see, as did Pico della Mirandola, that "we may have and possess, according to our desire and judgment, whatever place, whatever form, whatever function we shall desire." Our work in the next millennium is to integrate and transform the previous stages of evolution and thus to experience and express the unlimited power that is who and what we are when we are consciously attuned to the divine Will.

We express our greatest power not by exercising our personal willpower, but by *surrendering* to a Power greater than ourselves. This Power is referenced by many names throughout the world—the will of God, the will of Allah, the *Tao*, the *Dharma*—but always the meaning is essentially the same. As we let go of our egocentric desires and surrender to this divine Will, we find that we begin to change in a way not possible through personal effort alone. Not only do *we* change, but our world changes as well. As we learn to "conquer ourselves," we become a vehicle for the unlimited power of the universe to flow through us.

An example of a man who was such a vehicle is Mahatma Gandhi, who freed his homeland of two centuries of foreign rule without firing a shot. Gandhi writes: "There comes a time when an individual becomes irresistible and his action becomes all-pervasive in its effects. This comes when he reduces himself to zero."[5] Gandhi personified one who surrendered himself to the divine Will, and thus his power was virtually irresistible.

Surrendering to the flow of life, the Divine Plan, we eventually find a new source of power. Gradually, we begin to see that we are not living our life, but, rather, that our life is being lived through us. Life then takes on a flow, a rhythm, a synchronicity. With little effort, much is accomplished. Some would describe this as "living in the Tao"; for in the *Tao Te Ching* it is written:

> The Tao of heaven does not strive, and yet it overcomes.
> It does not speak, and yet is answered.
> It does not ask, yet is supplied with all its needs.
> It seems at ease, and yet it follows a plan. [6]

What is the plan that it follows? We could call it a "divine plan," or we could call it an "evolutionary imperative," which is essentially the same thing. It is the plan to which Teilhard referred when he envisioned evolution as the movement toward conscious oneness with God. We best prepare ourselves for this next step in our evolution when we surrender our personal will to the divine Will, when we surrender our limited human power to the unlimited, divine power.

CONSCIOUS SURRENDER

Let us remind ourselves that this act of surrender is not only an evolutionary imperative but may be essential to our survival on this planet. We are slowly awakening to the fact that all of humanity is, in a sense, one body on this planet. In a physical body each organ in the body, and each cell in the body, "surrenders" its will to a greater will, which is the intelligent life force in the body. When each organ and each cell—under the direction of the DNA molecule within the cell—is attuned to this life force, the body experiences a state of wholeness. When the organs or the cells are out of attunement with the life force, the body experiences a state of disease. Likewise, our world is in a state of wholeness when all beings in it are attuned to the Higher Will that is centered within us, just as the DNA molecule is centered within the nucleus of each cell. Conversely, our world is in a state of disease when the individuals in it are not attuned to the Higher Will but are enmeshed in egocentric desire. This is the cause of our suffering.

How does one surrender to the Higher Will? We are so accustomed to living from our personal will that we may feel, at first, confused by this process. We encounter what seems like a dilemma: If we "try to surrender," we are not surrendering! This is like "trying" to relax. We don't relax by trying, but by *not* trying, by letting go of personal effort. Surrender is much the same. We don't do it through effort, but, rather, by letting go of all personal "efforting."

Yet, our "letting go" must be deliberate and conscious; we do *not* surrender by simply becoming unconscious and falling asleep. Perhaps one way to discover what the experience of surrender is lies in looking at what it is *not*. It is *not* giving up or quitting. It is *not* resignation or despair. Surrender is *not* abdicating responsibility for the way we live our life. Surrender is a conscious "giving over" of oneself to something greater. It is living responsibly and skillfully by allowing a Higher Power to direct the course of our life.

Surrendering to the Higher Power does not necessarily mean that we sit and wait for God to do something for us or that we always wait for God to tell us what to do. A skillful sailor does not simply hoist the sails and make the wind responsible for directing the boat's course. The sailor uses the wind to power his boat by "surrendering" to the wind in a skillful way. Likewise, an expert canoeist surrenders her canoe to the flow of the river, yet remains alert and responsible for cooperating with that flow.

Being "surrendered" does not mean being a "doormat" for others to walk upon. We can say and do what is necessary to protect and assert ourselves in the world. Being surrendered means that we don't try to control and orchestrate the flow of our life; we let life unfold. We ask for what we want; we voice our opinion when appropriate, and we act when we need to act—but we are not attached to results.

DIVINE WILL BE DONE

Being "surrendered" means making a conscious choice to live while being constantly guided by the statement: "Not my will, but Thine be done." It means being in the world in a way in which we speak and act responsibly, but always within the context of "Thy will be done" (Mt. 26:42 RSV). We predicate all of our decisions upon the premise of "Thy will be done." We surrender all of our desires to "Thy will be done."

An important element in living consciously surrendered to the Higher Will is becoming aware of how we resist life as it unfolds—becoming aware of when we are subconsciously saying "not Thy will but *mine* be done." Some symptoms of this resistance are fear, anger, condemnation, and stubbornness. Physically, resistance may appear as tension and rigidity in the body. When we become aware of these experiences, it is helpful to relax as best we can, to close our eyes, to breathe deeply, and to say "Thy will be done" (as often as necessary!).

How do we know God's will? The truth is, we may not always consciously know. We may not hear voices or see "signs and wonders" telling us God's will. But as we pray for guidance, practice listening in the silence of meditation, and continue to affirm: *"Thy will be done,"* we can be assured that indeed, it is being done. Even if, through erroneous perception or poor judgment, we make what seem like mistakes, we will find ourselves living in a state of grace that somehow brings us back "on course." Remember, *surrender* means that *we* are not doing the work; it is being done *through* us.

Following divine Will is sometimes more about how we do something rather than what we do. God may not care whether we plant roses or petunias in our garden, but God does care about the attitude with which we perform the task. Are we doing it with a consciousness of mindfulness, caring, and a reverence for life, or are we seeing it as a chore to be completed so that our yard may look better and impress the neighbors?

One way to discover the divine Will for your life is to explore your soul's deepest desire—the desire of your heart. In *Lessons in Truth*, Dr. Emilie Cady writes, "Desire in the heart is always God tapping at the door of your consciousness."[7] We are here on earth—individually and collectively—to express God's Will. Humanity, as a species, is part of a divine plan that is seeking expression through the process of evolution. We, as individuals, likewise have divine plans that are unique to each of us. No one can tell us exactly what that plan is. Only we know, for it is hidden deep within our hearts. Only through listening to the heart in meditation, through the practice of self-awareness, through a commitment to fulfill our destiny, do we discover and fulfill our divine plan.

As we more fully surrender to the divine Will, we eventually find that our personal will is in perfect alignment with the greatest good for all life. Ultimately, our will and God's Will become as one. We find no difference between that which brings us true joy and that which serves the greater good for everyone and everything.

Within each soul, a divine plan guides its evolution. Within the collective soul of humanity, a divine plan directs the path of our evolution. The evolutionary design to which Teilhard, Hubbard, and others have alluded is a divine intelligence operating throughout all of creation. The same Intelligence that has created the universe, the earth, and the life forms on earth is God's Will at work in you right now. The same Intelligence which enables me to write these words and which enables you to read them is at work guiding us through the next step in our evolution. Just as a skillful canoeist aligns the canoe with the swiftest flow in the river, as we live centered in God's Will, we are aligning ourselves with the divine plan as it continuously flows and unfolds in and through each of us.

When we are spiritually asleep, when we are willful, when we are motivated by fear and anger, we are moving against the flow—caught in a back eddy, stuck in our own sense of separateness. As we let go, as we pay attention to the prompting of our soul, and as we trust the divine plan at work in our life, we move into harmony with the spirit of evolution that inexorably carries us—collectively and individually—forward into the next stage of the process leading to Omega: conscious oneness with God.

We see that our present crisis, with all its dangers, carries with it an unprecedented opportunity. Building upon thousands of years of human history and millions of years of evolution, we now stand poised on the threshold of a quantum leap in consciousness. An essential part of this readiness lies in mastering our use of the power that we have been given. Only then will we be ready to fulfill our potential for a greater power. The key to mastering our use of power lies in surrendering our personal power to a Higher Power; to become, individually and collectively, a vehicle for the only power in the universe—God, the Good, Omnipotent.

XII

187

XXI

> **Robert Brumet** is chairperson of Pastoral Studies and Skills for Unity School for Religious Studies at Unity Village, Missouri. Ordained in 1980, Robert served ministries in Evansville, Indiana, and Overland Park, Kansas, before joining the faculty in 1989. He received a master of science degree from the University of Toledo in Toledo, Ohio.

Robert has been featured in *Unity Magazine* and has authored the book *Finding Yourself in Transition: Using Life's Changes For Spiritual Awakening.* He has also created the audiocassette *Life Transitions: Growing Through Change.* Robert is working on a book on healing as part of the Unity Movement Advisory Council's continuing *Quest* series.

When his teaching schedule allows, Rev. Brumet travels and gives lectures and workshops around the country. He also has a counseling practice.

CHAPTER XI

THE POWER OF RENUNCIATION

With the power to control our thoughts and feelings comes the power to release the ones we no longer wish to entertain. This power is called "renunciation" or "elimination."

This power of letting go, and as many like to add, of letting God, is essential for a healthy state of mind—and body. Renunciation is the power of cleansing, of giving up, of casting off. It is the power of giving and forgiving, and ultimately, it is the power of knowing true freedom and liberation.

Popular images notwithstanding, elimination is not a negative thing. Renunciation makes it possible for there to be new thoughts and a new life. So renunciation needs the power of will to choose what thoughts to release. Renunciation needs, once again, the powers of wisdom, love, and understanding in order to know what to eliminate and what to affirm. This balance of giving and receiving is essential. The capacity to affirm is actually of equal importance to that of release, or denial, and very much a necessary part of the power of renunciation.

Thaddaeus, called Jude in some versions of Luke, represents the power of renunciation. How interesting that the name *Jude*, the same as the name *Judas*, suggests that renunciation is like the power of life. However, renunciation is the means by which life redeems itself.

189

A New Heaven and New Earth

Rosemary Fillmore Rhea

In the year 2001, a momentous event will occur—the end of a one thousand-year cycle and the beginning of another. According to history, something really does happen when those thousand-year marks come around. Some churches believe that the turn of the century heralds the approach of the Apocalypse. Others see it as the true Age of Aquarius, the beginning of two thousand years of peace, wisdom, and universal harmony.

Webster defines *millennium* as "the thousand years mentioned in Revelation 20 during which holiness is to prevail and Christ is to reign on earth; a period of great happiness or perfect government or freedom from imperfection in human existence." Whatever our individual interpretation of the millennium may be, most would agree that there is something going on. The winds of change are blowing across the land. A revolutionary spirit is sweeping away old concepts, old boundaries, old perceptions. Change is evident everywhere. We see it in religion, in technology, in our social and political structure. Or, as Buffalo Springfield said back in the '60s, "Something's happening here, and what it is ain't exactly clear."

Cycles of Change

The energy of creation is at work, moving us forward into new dimensions of being. On one hand, we are excited about the future, but on another level we want to cling to the past. We want to hold on to those things that made us feel safe and secure. However, we can move forward only by releasing—by renouncing—those old concepts that keep us bound to our painful history.

If there is one thing history teaches us, it is that you cannot stuff progress back in a box. Galileo was forced to stop teaching that the world was round, but that did not make it flat.

Every change that has meant progress for humankind has caused a great furor in the beginning, and yet change is the keynote of life. All living things change. And many of the most wonderful changes in nature would seem terribly disturbing to the creatures going through them—if those creatures thought as we do. Can you envision what the crab might feel if it experienced human emotion when its skin was beginning to split down the back and it realized that its skin—its very own skin—had become too small? Can you imagine what the tadpole would say, if it had human powers of thought and speech, when it found its tail fading away and funny-looking legs sprouting out of its body?

What dismay might the larva of the monarch butterfly express if it were human, when its muscles grew heavy and it felt the urge to build its own coffin? What gives it the courage to seal itself into that coffin and compose itself for apparent death? It cannot know the exquisite, winged creature that will split the coffin and come forth. The crab, the tadpole, and the infant butterfly are creatures governed by the laws of nature, by instinct. They are in tune with the transforming energy of creation, so they flow with the natural cycles of life.

These cycles of creation move in and through our lives as well, but we as reasoning beings question, doubt, and struggle when the energy of change begins the transformation process in us. In his fa-

mous poem "To a Mouse," poet Robert Burns makes the point that
it is only we humans who question the changes of creation. He says
to the mouse whose home he has turned up with the plow:

> Still thou art blest, compared wi' me,
> The present only toucheth thee:
> But, och! I backward cast my e'e
> On prospects drear!
> An' forward, though I canna see,
> I guess an' fear!

If we could renounce those nervous glances backward and forward and instead trust the natural flow of life as the crab, the tadpole, and the butterfly do, how much easier our own transformation
would be!

A TIME FOR TRANSFORMATION

We are living in transformative times. Right now, the world is experiencing an evolutionary shift. The creative energy of the universe is stirring the minds and hearts of people everywhere,
demanding that we awaken to the possibilities of a "new heaven
and a new earth."

The latter part of the twentieth century has been a time of amazing advances in science, medicine, and technology. The scientific
breakthroughs made in the last hundred years would have seemed
so unbelievable in Jesus' time, they would never even have been
considered. If you had suggested such things as antibiotics, organ
transplants, space travel, television, computers, and fax machines
even a century ago, people would have ridiculed you, would have
thought you insane.

And now, as we enter a new century, the scientific projections for
the future are even more mind-boggling. Ralph Merkle, a leading re-

searcher at the Xerox Palo Alto Research Center, predicts that "this new age is closer than we think and . . . that it will perhaps be possible in fifteen to twenty years to have dominion over the material world—both inanimate and biological."

We are also experiencing a communications revolution. We are being inundated with information and entertainment coming to us through on-line computer services, satellite broadcasting, films, cable, radio talk shows, shopping networks, video games, and on and on.

The world is in our living room, and it is almost overwhelming. We are learning more about everything and everybody than we ever really wanted to know. Sometimes the breaking wave of technology is frightening. But I feel very fortunate to have known well a spiritual leader who would not have found it frightening at all.

My grandfather, Charles Fillmore, would have found it splendid and exhilarating. He never had to sorrow, like Robert Frost, "over the road not taken," because he loved untraveled roads. Our whole family used to take trips to the Ozarks when I was a child. And if a road looked untraveled and led off into the wilderness, my grandfather, with a gleam of anticipation in his eye would say, "Let's see where this road goes." Sometimes we would come to dead ends, but always we would discover wonderful things that we would have missed if we had stayed on the well-traveled highway.

He would have seen every advancement in technology as further proof that we have only begun to tap our infinite potential. The information highway would have been of particular interest to Charles Fillmore. He was always exploring new ways of sharing the Unity message. He was one of the first religious leaders to use radio, saying it was "opening up a new field of activity in the case of the spoken word." The unknown always beckoned Charles Fillmore.

If he were with us in body today, I know he would be enthusiastically "surfing the Web" and filling it with Unity's message. He was truly a spiritual frontiersman who was always exploring new ideas and new ways to do things.

OUR SEARCH FOR ANSWERS

Who am I? What is the purpose of life? These are soul cries that have echoed down through the centuries. Human beings have always been incredibly curious about the meaning of life, and now as never before, people are searching for meaning and purpose as they deal with living in an intimate and compact world.

And as we enter the twenty-first century, the pace quickens; a sense of urgency increases. With the advent of the information age, we are more cognizant that the challenges of the century are universal ones. It has become clear that we can no longer separate ourselves into exclusive societies. Isolation won't work in a world of instant communication, in a world of economic dependency, in a world where ecology is a universal responsibility. And so in a world that at times seems chaotic and out of control, our search for answers becomes more intense.

We know that technology cannot solve the human dilemma. It cannot teach us how to live in harmony with ourselves, our neighbors, and our earth. But it has brought us to the place where we realize that all people must learn to live in harmony with one another and our planet if we are to survive.

With the explosion of the first atomic bomb, our world changed forever. It was a defining moment in the history of civilization, the beginning of a new era in human consciousness. For the first time, people realized unequivocally that war was no longer an acceptable alternative for solving differences. Sometimes it seems that we have only exchanged one big war for a multitude of little ones, but the destructive power of nuclear weapons has indeed had a sobering influence on power politics.

In the 1960s, a shift in consciousness became very evident. It was the beginning of a different kind of a quest—an inward one. The realization that to change our world, we must first change ourselves, began to filter into human consciousness. Meditation, encounter groups, Eastern philosophies, Self-realization, and other new ways of thinking ushered in what was called by some the "Age of Aquarius."

A new vision, or perhaps an ancient one revisited, was articulated through the voices of the '60s. This cultural change was expressed in the music, in the art, and through the words of people like Dr. Martin Luther King, Jr. and others. We awakened to the possibilities of a world without war, a world where there is no hunger or racism or violence—a world where every child could look forward to living in unity, in harmony with one another and with the environment. We began to envision a new heaven and a new earth.

In those same '60s, when I was presenting the *Daily Word* program on television, I was invited to go on a tour arranged for media people to visit places in the news and to meet and interview world leaders. We made a film for the *Daily Word* programs and also for a half-hour documentary entitled *Around the World in Search of Faith*, which was shown on television stations across the country.

We photographed the closed border through which mainland refugees were leaking into Hong Kong, a divided and war-torn Jerusalem, strife in Vietnam, memorials where people had been killed at the Berlin Wall, and closed churches in Moscow. But the camera also found thousands bringing gifts of flowers to Gandhi's tomb, hopeful words from world leaders, and the wonderful faces of ordinary people. The film ended with the statement that although there were many walls in the world, there were also hopeful signs of bridges going up; and I recall being castigated by some people at that time for "Pollyanna thinking."

Looking back now, I see that we were not one bit too optimistic. The walls we photographed have all come down. Berlin is one city. There is a determined peace initiative going forward in the Middle East. Hong Kong is making an orderly transition as a part of China. The churches in Moscow are reopening. And all the "satellite" countries are whipping along in orbits of their own—not always smooth, but indisputably free ones.

Because I saw these changes for myself, I am convinced that however much we may stumble, our way is always upward. We would, of course, like to speed up the process, and we question what we need to do to bring forth a new world. Perhaps it is not so much what we need to do, as what we need to *stop* doing. Perhaps our first need is renunciation of those old ideas that keep us separated from one another and from God.

Universal Unity

Heretofore, the world's religions have provided the answers for our search for Truth. But religions have also been divisive. On the one hand, they have provided the inspiration that has awakened humankind to the spiritual dimension of life; on the other hand, they have been at the root of many of the conflicts that have plagued our civilization. If we are to bring forth the millennium as described in Revelation, we must begin expressing a transcendent spirituality that supersedes the bigotry of religiosity and is open to new ways of living and thinking which will plant the seeds for a new era of universal unity.

This is not to say we should all have the same belief system; on the contrary, it is the diversity of our quest that makes our search so mysterious and exciting. How boring it would be if we were all exactly the same! When we understand that the search for God is universal, it will perhaps be easier for us to release our religious and cultural biases.

The Moslem kneeling on his prayer rug, facing Mecca, has the same desire to know God as the Christian kneeling in the cathedral. The Hindu chanting her mantra by the Ganges is on the same search as the Jew bowing before the Wailing Wall. The Buddhist spinning the prayer wheel, the Shintoist before his holy shrine, the Native American honoring her ancestors—all are a part of the magnificent tapestry of life. And if we could see through the veils of time, we would perhaps discover that we have walked many paths in forgotten lifetimes.

There are dimensions beyond our knowing, and as citizens of a global society, we must learn to embrace our differences and celebrate our individuality. The spirituality of the twenty-first century must be inclusive rather than exclusive.

Renouncing our Grievances

Living in revolutionary times is not easy. The Chinese have a blessing that also serves as a curse: "May you live in interesting times!" Revolutions demand that we renounce those ideas and conceptions which keep us from moving forward. One of the most difficult things for us to do as members of the human species is to let go of old beliefs and perceptions. History has shown that we are often willing to live unhappy, limited lives—or even to die—rather than to change our beliefs, to see things in a new way, to release the old in favor of the new.

In the parts of the world where peace initiatives keep breaking down over and over again, it is the rehashing of past grievances (whether religious or ethnic) that continuously stirs the fire of revenge. Once revenge is accomplished, the opposing group wants the same thing, and the strife goes on. The only possible solution is to renounce vengeance. It is only through forgiveness that we can find peace and freedom.

It is only through the releasing of past injustices, past prejudices, past hurts that we can ever move forward. Gandhi said that if everyone practiced the eye-for-an-eye morality, soon "the whole world would be blind." Perhaps it is natural to want to do to others what they have done to us, but it is not good enough. It is not the way of spiritual advancement. It was certainly not the way of Jesus.

It was his way to love the enemy, turn the other cheek, go the second mile. He could renounce "natural" feelings in favor of spiritual ones. Two thousand years ago, he told us how to break the chain of recurrent strife and showed us the perfect example in the way he dealt with his own life. He held out the promise of a perfect world.

Almost a century ago, another spiritual leader was envisioning a "new heaven and a new earth." Charles Fillmore wrote in the "Renunciation" chapter of *The Twelve Powers of Man,* "The earth is slowly regaining its equilibrium and will in due season be restored to its pristine golden age."

But what is standing in the way of this miracle coming to pass? Only we are. Charles Fillmore wrote, "Man is the dominant thinking and character-giving force of the earth, and he has made it a place of desolation when it should be a paradise."

He goes on to give us a three-step plan for our spiritual progress by comparing the Pharisees, John the Baptist, and Jesus. He wrote that "the personalities of Scripture represent mental attitudes in the individual." Jesus is the fully-enlightened spiritual consciousness. John the Baptist represents the intellect in its transition from the natural to the spiritual plane, willing to give up the old and advocating a general denial through water baptism, which stands for mental cleansing.

The Pharisees have not entered this transition, but cling stubbornly to the old customs and traditions, refusing even to admit that any change might be needed. "If you are clinging to any idea that in any way prevents your eyes from seeing the millennium here and now," warns Charles Fillmore, "you are a Pharisee; you are crying, 'Beelzebub,' whenever you say 'crank' of the one who has caught sight of the spiritual mountaintops now glistening in the sun of the new age."

The lesson of the Pharisees is renunciation, not just of old ideas or old wrongs, but of any attempt to sort out experience intellectually. We must deny before we can affirm, just as we must raze an old building before we can erect a new one in its place. "What man forms that is evil," wrote Charles Fillmore, "he must unform before he can take the coveted step up the mountain of the ideal. Here enters the factor that dissolves the structures that are no longer useful; this factor in metaphysics is known as denial. . . . It is simply the absence of the impulse that constructs and sustains." We do not have to struggle against what is wrong; we only have to take from it the support of our thoughts and words.

All our positive and determined efforts to make our lives and the world better cannot succeed until we make the preliminary move of renunciation, of formally and voluntarily giving up whatever old ideas we are holding and presenting ourselves as a *tabula rasa*, a clean page, giving *carte blanche* for spiritual Truth to be written in. This is the meaning of Jesus' saying that we must become "as a little child" to enter the kingdom of heaven; the mind of the child is just such a clean page.

If you are crying out for God, but feel you cannot reach Him and cannot make a difference in your world, you are John the Baptist crying in the wilderness. He stands for the perception of Truth that prepares the way for Spirit, but he departs from the line of harmony in practicing condemnation of the senses, of his own errors and those of others. His lesson to us is that we must not condemn, but forgive and accept.

FORGIVENESS—A SURE REMEDY

Charles Fillmore wrote in a pamphlet called *A Sure Remedy* that if we would take a half-hour every night and mentally forgive everyone who has hurt us or caused us pain, it would cure every ill the flesh is heir to. He suggested that we see people as they really are in Spirit—evolving souls, just as we are. And as we forgive, we are forgiven.

Self-condemnation is just as restricting, if not even more so, than condemnation of others. Everyone makes mistakes. We do things we wish we hadn't done; we "mess up." But the past is past, and in

Truth there are no mistakes, just lessons to learn. Each new day, each new moment, is the opportunity to choose again. The greatest gift we can give ourselves and our world is the gift of forgiveness.

We spoke earlier of the need for nations to forgive; it is just as important in each individual life. We don't go forward to be the person we want to be as long as we hold on to the person we once were. Guilt binds and confines. Forgiveness frees us to experience a creative future—the "new heaven and new earth."

We may think that what we do individually does not matter in the great scheme of things. Indeed, we may not have control over the games played by the power brokers of the world. We may not be able to do much about the rise and fall of the dollar or what happens in the Middle East. But every one of us has an important mission to fulfill in the evolution of human consciousness.

The Coming World Harmony

The world we are experiencing today is the result of our collective consciousness, and if we want a new world, each of us must start taking responsibility for helping create it.

Dr. Arnold Toynbee once said that the salvation of the world will be the coming of a great spiritual leader—not a politician, not a statesman, not an intellectual scholar, but a person of Spirit. As twenty-first-century citizens, we must take Dr. Toynbee's prediction one step further; the salvation of the world lies not with one spiritually illumined person, but with each one of us.

In the past, we have always been looking for something or someone out there to save us. But to experience a new heaven and a new earth, each one of us must put the weight of our personal conviction, our thought, our work, our energy, and our passion into creating them.

As we approach the millennium, we see that universal harmony is much more than a wish, a hope, or a dream. It is a necessity, and we must take on the responsibility of seeing it become a reality. In our desire to express creative ideas in the form of new technologies, new systems, and new modes of living, we have taken courses of action that have had dramatically destructive effects on one of God's most magnificent creations—planet Earth.

The Earth is our home, and we share this home with a vast array of different forms of life. Our incredible, God-given ability to create must be directed and guided with Christlike compassion as we consider the effects that our efforts to improve the human condition have on all forms of life on Earth and on the Earth itself.

Charles Fillmore said that human beings are the pinnacle of God's creation, and as such we must consider the well-being of all life. It has become necessary for us to recognize a new dimension of our creative power—the ability and responsibility to create in harmony with the needs of the Earth and all forms of life upon it. This will require that we go beyond merely seeing the divine in human life, but that we acknowledge and honor the divine in all forms of life as well. Centuries ago, the mystic Meister Eckhart wrote:

> Apprehend God in all things, for God is in all things. Every single creature is full of God, and is a book about God. Every creature is a word of God. If I spend enough time with the tiniest creature—even a caterpillar—I would never have to prepare a sermon. So full of God is every creature.

In the new millennium we must put into action the acknowledgment that God is equally present in all life by demonstrating respect for all life. I believe that the same technologies which we have used to create so many incredible breakthroughs for humanity in this century will be used for the benefit of all forms of life in the new millennium. While we have often hurt the Earth in the name of progress and technological advancement, in the new millennium we as a race will renounce this belief in the dominion of human needs in favor of a much more compassionate viewpoint. We will recognize and embrace the divinity in all of life, and we will use our advanced creative abilities to nurture and support all of creation, rather than to destroy some parts of it in favor of others.

A New Heaven and a New Earth

Barbara Marx Hubbard says that the twenty-first century could be the "beginning of the millennium in which universal spirituality is born, the time when the awareness that every one of us is created by the same Source, is inheritor of the same power, and is needed for the evolution of the whole body." This is a magnificent vision, and if enough of us dedicate ourselves to helping bring it forth, we will see the pendulum swing and a new heaven and a new earth will come into being.

However, great visions can seem almost overwhelming when we are trying to make a living, keep our family together, and do all of the things that need to be done in our complex society. We can think globally, but we live locally, and the new world must first be born in us. This is where we come to the lesson of Jesus: We are spiritual beings, and nothing is impossible to us when we practice the presence of God.

It is most important to take time each day to experience moments of peace—of silence. This is something I learned from my grandfather. Wherever he was when he had a time when he was not involved in some activity, he would meditate. He called it "going into the silence." It was so natural for him that you never thought it strange or unusual. In fact, as a kid, I thought everyone's grandfather practiced the silence—until my friends assured me that theirs didn't!

The silence was my grandfather's answer to health problems, to writings that condemned his teachings, to a payroll there was not enough money to meet, to joy he needed to share and give thanks for. And the silence never failed him.

I have always remembered this and sought the silence in my own life. In today's noisy and insistent world, it is hard to find room for silence, but it is absolutely necessary if we are to keep our focus and find our way. Going into the silence is a skill we learn by consciously practicing the presence of God, by inserting quiet moments wherever we can fit them into our busy schedule.

When we are standing in line, waiting at a stoplight, having a coffee break, we can make these holy moments, God moments. When we center ourselves in the silence, we are not only helping ourselves, we are contributing to peace in the world.

It is also important to make time for joy. Charles Fillmore was a spiritual leader, but there was nothing stuffy or repressive about him. He loved life and he loved people, and he made you feel good about just being alive. He celebrated everything—birthdays, holidays, anything that happened. He enjoyed the band concerts and Saturday night dances at Unity Village. When Unity was still in its Kansas City offices, if it was an especially beautiful day, "Papa Charlie," as we called him, would load all the workers up in buses and take them for a day at Unity Farm. His faith was full of joy.

Another thing I learned from my grandfather was to celebrate our individualism. There is no one just like you anywhere in the world, so why waste time trying to emulate other people? You have something to give the world that no one else can give. You are important to life, and the moment you appreciate yourself and celebrate yourself, you will discover a new sense of purpose and meaning.

It is not necessary for a person to be a rocket scientist or a Mother Teresa to be effective. What is necessary is that we express our soul gifts in the area where we have chosen to live our life—as the old hymn says it, "Brighten the corner where you are."

The changes in the world have become so vast and so rapid that subconsciously or consciously we may feel our individuality is at

XII

203

XXI

risk. We fear the "I" in us will be lost in a society that no longer needs our particular skill or expertise. But this is not the Truth of us. We are made for transcendence. If we are awakened to what is real, to what is enduring, we will never give up on ourselves or on life.

It has been said that we are living in a world of permanent change. And this is true. The only permanence is in impermanence. Everything changes. Life is a series of endings and new beginnings. And when we understand that change is vital to our growth and unfoldment, we will trust that God is guiding and loving us as we go through all the transformations that are necessary for our total evolution.

We cannot be separate from God. Our life is not a separate thing. We are one with all the life there ever has been or ever will be. Every thought we think, every word we speak, every action we take, affects the whole. It was Frances Thompson who wrote, "Thou canst not pluck a flower without troubling a star." We should never, never discount our impact on the universe.

We were born to create, and we always have the choice of whether we will create for good or for evil. And the wondrous thing is that with every new moment we have the opportunity of choosing again.

One day when enough of us awaken to the infinite power within us—"Christ in you, the hope of glory" (Col. 1:27)—we will see a world we have never seen before: a world in which no one is hungry or in need, a world in which the fortunes now spent for arms will be spent for people, a world in which the fear of nuclear war has become only a chapter in the book of history.

There is nothing visionary about this world. It is for us to see with our own eyes and grasp with our own minds and hearts so that we may bring it into expression. John saw it some two thousand years ago:

"And I saw a new heaven and a new earth: for the first heaven and the first earth are passed away . . . . And I heard a great voice out of the throne saying, Behold, the tabernacle of God is with men, and he shall dwell with them . . . and be their God: and he shall wipe away every tear from their eyes; and death shall be no more . . . the first things are passed away. And he that sitteth on the throne said, Behold, I make all things new. And he saith, Write: for these words are faithful and true. And he said unto me, They are come to pass." (Rev. 21:1, 3–5 ASV).

As we continue to envision a world where all people are safe, well, and abundantly supplied, where fulfilling work and creative expression are the rule rather than the exception, and where the needs of all creatures and of the earth itself are honored at the same level as the needs of humanity, we shall indeed one day see that these things "are come to pass."

XII

205

XXI

The granddaughter of Unity co-founders Charles and Myrtle Fillmore, **Rosemary Fillmore Rhea** serves as a member of the Retreat Department of Unity School of Christianity at Unity Village, Missouri.

Rosemary, ordained a Unity minister in 1980, founded the Myrtle Fillmore Center, presently in Prairie Village, Kansas, and is an active speaker for Unity throughout the country and the world. Through a series of open-forum meetings, she was instrumental in bringing Unity to the former Soviet Union, where there are now two study groups, one in Moscow and one in Pustchino.

Rosemary Rhea began a 25-year career in multimedia in Hollywood, California. Upon her return to Kansas City, she produced and hosted radio station WHB's education talk show *Young Ideas*. After that, she directed and hosted Unity's five-minute television broadcast, *The Daily Word*, for twelve years. With her late husband, Ralph Rhea, she initiated the public-service program entitled *The Word*, which was on more than one thousand radio and television stations.

The coproducer of three documentary films, *Around the World in Search of Faith; Charles Fillmore: American Mystic;* and *Unity, a School of Christianity*, Rosemary has been listed in *Who's Who of American Women*. She has been actively involved in the International Relations Council, American Federation of Television and Radio Artists, White House Conference for Education for Missouri, and American Women in Radio and Television Broadcasting.

THE POWER OF ORDER

At last we come to the least, and that deserves an explanation. Obviously, order is not least, for order is the harmony of law, logic, and adjustment. Order, like our first power—love—is harmony. Order is the music of the spheres as well as the inner science that makes the DNA of our cells as carefully constructed as the spiral arms of some distant galaxy.

The power of order is the power of relationship, of the perceived harmony between things and processes. It is linked with faith, the perceiving power; with will, the choosing power; with renunciation, the releasing power. In many ways, order is the other half of renunciation, the half to do with affirmation. Order is the affirming power, the recognizing power that God is in charge and all is well. In New Thought, we often say, "Divine Order" when we mean to affirm that God's will is being done.

James of Alphaeus represents order. He is not to be confused with James of Zebedee, who symbolizes wisdom, yet the discerning power of wisdom has much to do with choosing divine order. James of Alphaeus is sometimes called "James the Less" to distinguish him from the other, and that's why, in one sense only, order is last and least!

James of Alphaeus is also sometimes thought of as Jesus' brother (Gal. 1:19). Jesus, the Christ, represents the complete, perfect wholeness of the God-realized human being. James, then, can be seen as resembling Jesus. Order, then, brings us close to knowing the harmony, the wholeness, of our spiritual nature. It, however, like the others, needs to be in balance with the other eleven powers.

Without the balance, order is the lesser. With the balance, we come to be one with the Elder Brother, the Christ.

Discovery of a New Ordering of the Future

Barbara Marx Hubbard

My very first memory is sitting strapped into my high chair in New York City, the early morning sun beaming through the window, banging the tray table with my fists, scattering crumbs everywhere, proclaiming at the top of my lungs, "Law and Order!" And being told to keep quiet and eat my breakfast!

Looking back upon that little two-year-old girl as I write this article, I see that her affirmation and request to the universe, made at the very end of one phase of human history (1932) has indeed guided my search for the last sixty years, in an attempt to fulfill the intention set forth by that child. I would briefly like to trace my own discovery of a new ordering of the future and how this implicate order might now guide the conscious evolution of self and society. (It is preferable to change the word *order* into a verb rather than a noun. We are discerning the ordering process, rather than a static "order.")

The discovery process began for me as a young girl, with a deep, intuitive sense that something great was coming from all this power of the modern world, something new, something beyond material success, yet based on our newly-won freedom, affluence, and capacity attained since the advent of democracy and the technologi-

209

cal/industrial revolution. But what was it? I could see the destructive potential of the power, as in the atomic bomb (and later in environmental degradation and social alienation). But what is the positive meaning of these powers? What are positive images of the future equal to our emerging spiritual, social, and scientific/technological potential? I asked.

In my search I picked up a Viking Portable on the world religions and read the great statements from the New Testament:

> "Behold I show you a mystery: We shall not all sleep, we shall all be changed. In a moment, in the twinkling of an eye, at the last trump, for the trumpet shall sound and the dead will be raised imperishable, and we shall all be changed" (1 Cor. 15:51, 52).

> Then I saw a new heaven and a new earth . . . . And I saw the holy city, New Jerusalem, coming down from God out of Heaven . . . and God shall wipe away all tears from their eyes, and there shall be no more death, neither sorrow, nor crying, neither shall there be any more pain; for the former things are passed away" (Rev. 21:1, 2, 4).

There. That was *it*! The basis of hope, the purpose of our power is radical transformation, genuine newness, metamorphosis, a quantum jump beyond the current human condition. At the age of sixteen, excitement arose in my heart, and I looked around for the nearest church.

I found the local Episcopal church, met the minister, and asked him my questions: "Did Jesus really do all this? Will we? How shall we all be changed? How do you get from Scarsdale, New York, to the New Jerusalem? What is the process?" The priest clearly did not know. (And I was undoubtedly a bit overbearing!)

Then I married and had five children, losing the questions in the massive and loving effort to reproduce the species. I did not surface for fifteen years, in the early sixties, when the search for meaning and an order I could follow in my own life led me to the discoveries that form the foundation of my understanding and the logic of hope.

THE DISCOVERY OF THE PATTERN

It was through the Jesuit paleontologist Fr. Teilhard de Chardin that I first made the discovery of the pattern, or ordering, which can guide us in the twenty-first century. In his book *The Phenomenon of Man,* he wrote that a transcendent order is revealed as "the recurring pattern in the process of creation." The invisible hand of God is made visible through the discovery of the mysterious, highly improbable and incredibly transformative journey from the origin of the physical universe, through the formation of subatomic particles, atoms, molecules, galaxies, planets, cells, multicellular creatures, ecologies, humans . . . to us now going around the turn of the spiral again.

He described the pattern as "the Law of Complexity/Consciousness." As a system becomes more complex, it undergoes a *quantum jump* in consciousness and freedom, from molecule to cell to multicellular animals to humans—the most complex organisms on Earth. A quantum jump is a radical discontinuity, a phase change that produces genuine newness unpredictable from the former state, yet, as we can see from the recurring pattern, one that involves higher consciousness and greater freedom of choice and action.

Now, Teilhard saw that planet Earth is a living organism. It is complexifying rapidly as a whole system. All our functional systems are integrating—economic, environmental, communicative, defensive. We are all *in fact* members of one body—organically and functionally as well as spiritually. At some point, Teilhard felt, this organism as a whole would "get its collective eyes." He called this next turn of the spiral "Omega," or "the Christification of the Earth."

It would be a time when each of us, as members of this living body, would experience ourselves, as St. Paul once put it, empathetically connected with one another and the whole Earth as one body.

> "For just as the body is one and has many members, and all the members of the body, though many, are one body, so it is with Christ. . . . Indeed, the body does not consist of one member but of many."
>
> —1 Cor. 12:12, 14

We are all to become, experientially, members of the living body of Christ, each unique, each equally valuable and needed. What mystics of all cultures and traditions had experienced in flashes of light was, according to Teilhard, a precognitive experience of what is already true, yet has not been collectively experienced.

Later, Peter Russell, in *The Global Brain*, hypothesized that it takes approximately ten billion atoms to make a cell and ten billion cells to make a brain. He noted that one more doubling of our population, expected in this living generation, will bring the population to ten billion people, the carrying capacity of the Earth. Perhaps, he said, it takes that many neurons to create the spiritual density for members of this body to actually feel themselves to be one whole system. He writes in *The White Hole in Time*:

> Could it be that, in much the same way as the density of matter in a sufficiently massive star is to become a black hole in space, the density of a self-conscious species—should it be sufficiently full of love—is a 'spiritual supernova'[?] Is this what we are accelerating towards? . . . A white hole in time?[1]

These observations confirm the revelations of Jesus and Paul that a time would come in history when we would all be changed. Teilhard had discovered the recurring pattern, the implicate order of evolution. His discovery provided me with the *logic* of my intuitive hope that something great is coming. It affirmed the vision of the New Jerusalem, as the next stage of evolution. Of course, the "former things are passed away." That's what happens. There is no more early Earth before the biosphere. There are no more dinosaurs. Perhaps there will be no more self-centered Homo sapiens. We are a transitional species evolving toward that higher, divine human which has been embodied by the great *avatars* of the human race and which is being activated in millions of us now, as the whole planetary body enters its "crisis of birth," its time of trial, when the whole must coordinate and integrate itself as one living system.

This tendency toward holism appears to be prepatterned, prepotential, but not predetermined for any one species or individual. There is freedom in the system. In fact, freedom increases with complexity, as Jan Smuts first pointed out in *Holism and Evolution*. As we move up the chain of life, freedom of choice increases. The future is not an inevitability, but a contingency. We can see that in the human dilemma today. We have ever more power to destroy or to create. As Brian Swimme puts it in *The Universe Story*, "The universe lives on a knife's edge." It matters what each of us thinks, intends, and does. Yet the tendency in the whole universal process that is expressed through each of us as individuals is for our own self-evolution, our own emergence as higher beings through our participation in a more complex or synergistic whole. The evolutionary selection process favors our tendency toward spirituality, universality, inclusivity, connectedness, morality, and "cosmic consciousness." Words fail us in describing the next stage of human evolution, for, as far as I know, it has not yet fully happened anywhere to anyone on this Earth. It has not been the "fullness of time," as Jesus said.

XII

213

XXI

A Higher Quality Human

But from the point of view of the discovery of order in the twenty-first century, the evolutionary selection process and what we have called the "will of God" seem related, if not identical. Both are pressuring or guiding us to become a higher quality human in order to survive. We are reinforced when we attune to the deeper pattern of creation for higher consciousness and greater freedom, and we are disempowered and even destroyed when we separate from that tendency, especially now, when we hold the power to destroy this world as we know it or to cocreate a future of immeasurable possibilities.

Instead of thinking of the inner aspiration for something new and great as a foolish, unsubstantiated longing—as portrayed by the existentialism, scientific materialism, or nihilism rampant at that time—I saw that our innermost, secret motivations are an expression of the very same ordering tendency that was, is now, and ever will be creating the universe! The Force *is* with us.

This is a fifteen-billion-year trend. In my case, my life took on meaning. The "I" of identity shifted from my agnostic, existentialist, and morose view that "I" was a meaningless bit of flesh and blood in a universe going down to an inevitable heat death from increased entropy or disorder (the current, materialistic, scientific view). "I," each of us as an "I," is an expression of the whole process of creation. In our genes are all the generations come alive now. Our atoms, molecules, cells, organs, and early brain have the memory of the whole story of creation. We are awakening to that story as our own birth story. When we remember who we are, as James Redfield tells us in *The Tenth Insight*, we remember our "birth vision," our individual soul purpose. When we join together with others, we can intuit the larger story of creation and the vision of our collective potential, our shared birth vision, toward which we are now tending.

This collective vision is vital now, for it magnetizes us toward it, to fulfill it.

> The key aspect of this Vision . . . is not the mere experience of it, although that's hard enough. It's how we *project* this Vision of the future, how we *hold it* for the rest of humanity.[2]

If we believe that the future is somehow doomed, that we are headed for catastrophe, our motivation is nipped in the bud, and we are disempowered—for as we see the future, so we act, and as we act, so we become. We are neither optimists nor pessimists. We are potentialists. We see the reality of our potential and are moved to fulfill it. If we do not remember who we are and what we can be, the process of creation cannot align itself fully with us and we are relatively disempowered by our lack of awareness.

THE ORDERING TENDENCY OF EVOLUTION

I was enormously reinforced and uplifted by this sense of the pattern, of the ordering tendency of evolution. I understand that God has two aspects, the "eternal" and the "evolving." Most mystics of the past have awakened to the eternal aspect of the Creator, that which is changeless, permanent, the field of all possibilities. But now, in this very generation, an equally real aspect of God is being shown to us through the discovery of the new cosmology brought to us by the young eyes of science. Our telescopes peer backwards in time to the beginning of the creation, sensing from faint impulses of the earliest light the fabulous story of our creation from the beginning to now. This process cannot be fully explained by the Darwinian mechanistic view claiming that errors in the copy mechanisms of the genetic code, combined with natural selection, created all this.

The probability of even one string of amino acids forming itself by chance is extremely small. The process of evolution reveals an unfoldment, an implicate order, as David Bohm called it, an ordering, design, and direction whose fruit is ever higher consciousness and greater freedom through more complex or synergistic order. (This view is controversial and certainly not yet accepted by many scientists, yet there are those who are both scientific and open to the awareness of design in evolution.)

The consciousness required to fully live the twenty-first century is a combination of the eternal and the evolving aspects of God. We can access this form of consciousness at the core of our being as the Eternal, the ever-present Oneness, the Presence of God. This is our center, our Source. Centered in Source, we recognize that we are unique expressions of the process of creation and have a vital role to play in the creation.

We see that each of us is called from within to stabilize ourselves as cocreative humans, humans capable of accessing the eternal aspect of God and simultaneously awakening to the evolving aspect—humans expressing our God-given creative essence as Spirit-in-action in the world.

The very best training grounds we have for this new ordering on the personal level is found in the "cocreative" teachings, as in Unity and in Religious Science. These teachings understand the nature of humans from the spiritual/evolutionary perspective. Each of us is a spiritual person, created by this whole process of creation, each of us is an expression of the divine Love-Intelligence. Each of us, through our awareness, intention, affirmation, and action, is actually cocreating our own reality right now. From the evolutionary point of view, these truths do not represent a new religion, but the evolution of religion. Unity calls us to do and be as Jesus—that is, the next stage of human evolution incarnated, embodied, and demonstrated in our lives.

The fact is, then, we do have great teachings and examples of spiritual evolution, from every tradition. We also are advancing on the technological front. We are sublime cocreators in our understanding of the atom, the gene, the brain. As engineers we are fabulous. Artistically, we are fabulous. But socially, we lag way behind ourselves. Society as currently designed is a living disaster for billions of people, who are starving, sick, ignorant, and in pain, and is even more so for other species and our common environment. It is impossible to be an evolving human in what seems to be a dying world. And our technology can be and so often is misused for destructive ends, given social structures that encourage competition and warfare. What do we need to do to bring our social evolution up to the level in which our spiritual and technological capacities can be fulfilled? We must turn our attention to the social present and see how the ordering tendencies of evolution can be used as guidelines to cocreate a society equal to our full potential.

Visions of a Positive Future

A first step to manifest the ordering tendency of evolution in our society is to bring forth visions of the desirable future to move toward. As images of personal wellness heal us personally, so images of social wellness help to heal and evolve us socially. Let's take a moment now to imagine ourselves at the next stage of our evolution— a wiser, more mature, universal humanity. What is the *future present* aborning among us now? This vision is conceived by connecting our emerging capacities and peak capabilities and imagining them operating harmoniously as a new norm.

The first emergent capacity is ancient. It is higher consciousness itself. We can become stabilized in a universal, cosmic, Christ-centered, Buddha-minded, whole-centered consciousness. As we remember that evolution raises consciousness and freedoms, we become *conscious* evolutionaries, capable of guiding our own process of creation through deeper attunement with the patterns (and/or Presence of God) that are creating us.

Next, as our universal consciousness stabilizes, we become self-healing and even self-regenerating humans, as Charles and Myrtle Fillmore so powerfully taught. We have seen the miracles of healing that Jesus did, and we know through demonstration that we can do as he did. A combination of the healing arts and advancing medical technology leads to the possibility of extended, regenerating life, not only on this Earth, but eventually in the universe beyond our home planet as we learn to become a planetary and then a galactic species.

These are not merely technological achievements. They are expressions of a bioevolutionary advance as important as when life came out of the sea onto the dry and barren planet. Who could have predicted the verdant biosphere and human culture in those muddy pools so long ago? Who among us can foresee the possibilities of a species gaining universal consciousness and extended life and becoming physically universal in a cosmos of billions and billions of galaxies! We can already live and work beyond our planet. We are now extraterrestrial beings ourselves. In our solar system alone are materials of a thousand Earths, including metals, minerals, and solar energy. If we grow "normally," we will soon have access to nonterrestrial resources. There is no energy shortage, no space shortage, no shortage whatsoever for a universal humanity. Both spiritually and physically we are not limited to the current stage of terrestrial, self-centered humanity.

As we are developing a cosmic, universal consciousness on the inner plane and on the physical dimension, so we are also advancing toward universal intelligence. Through our extended global brain we are "growing" an electronic nervous system. Faxes, phones, the Internet, Web sites, mass media are linking us together as members of one living planetary body. Our intelligence, both inner and outer, is maturing at an exponential rate.

XII
___
218
___
XXI

Now let us imagine the individual child born into this maturing "noosphere," the thinking layer—beyond the geosphere, the hydrosphere, and the biosphere—composed of our culture, technologies, and social systems. This matured noosphere renders each of us radically more powerful than premodern humans. Not as single individuals but only as members of this larger body do we have the power of godlings. Through our collective capacities we can flash our images with the speed of light around the world. We can go to the moon. We can map all the genes in our body. We may be able to build atom by atom through nanotechnology, as nature does. We can intervene, for better or worse, in the process of evolution itself, building new life forms. We can blow up cities and build new worlds in space. This is a radical jump in capacity.

If it is true, as Margaret Mead once said, that even the greatest geniuses among us have only used 10 percent of their creative potential, then the 90 percent-untapped human potential is to be called forth in the maturing noosphere of the whole system. This new whole can be seen to include both Christ consciousness and Christ-like capacities gained through our collective social and technological abilities. When we learn to combine our science of mind (spiritual growth) with our science of matter (technological advances) we are already in a quantum jump, a species-wide metamorphosis. In fact, we are not all sleeping. We are now all being changed. In the twinkling of a cosmic eye, we are seeing the unfolding of a universal humanity.

I believe the vision of a New Jerusalem is a prescientific, early-human intuition of what it will be like when our spiritual, social, and scientific capacities mature in alignment with the ordering processes of creation. Holding such visions of our own personal and social evolutionary potential acts as a magnet to pull us forward, reinforcing our motivation to transcend and encouraging the intuition of radical newness emerging through us now.

XII

219

XXI

A New Social Architecture
for the New Millennium

The question is: How do we move toward that future on the social frontier? or How does the ordering process guide us in our development of a society that fosters human maturity and spiritual elevation? As Ralph Abraham writes in *Chaos, Gaia, Eros*:

> Here is the crux of world problems. Its evolution—*cultural evolution*, or *sociogenesis*—is subject to the laws of general evolution theory. As we learn those laws from comparative studies of the histories of geogenesis, biogenesis, and noogenesis, we may develop the capability to guide our own sociogenesis, and to participate in the creation of our own future. This points to a new science of the future, a true social science, with mathematical models and observational laws, with understanding and wisdom, and with a basis in history and social philosophy.[3]

One of the ordering keys to the new society lies in a single word: *synergy*. According to the *American Heritage Dictionary*, *synergy* is, biologically, "the action of two or more substances, organs, or organisms to achieve an effect of which each is individually incapable." Theologically, it is "the doctrine that regeneration is effected by the combination of human will and divine grace."

Nature has been forming synergistic systems for billions of years. Holism, the tendency to form whole systems out of separate parts, is the nature of reality. It is the great tradition! It is the way quantum jumps occur. Synergy occurs in a whole system when separate parts come together to form a new whole that is different from, unpredictable from, and greater than the sum of its parts. All bodies are synergistic systems. There is no way anyone could imagine the human body from an array of its separate organs laid out on a table! Can we imagine a whole synergistic planetary society? Not by adding up the parts, but we do have clues, because we can see how synergy has worked in the past and apply that knowledge to society now.

This concept of social synergy was developed by the anthropologist Ruth Benedict who distinguished between low and high synergy:

> I shall speak of cultures with low synergy where the social structure provides for acts which are mutually opposed and counteractive, and cultures with high synergy where it provides for acts which are mutually reinforcing. . . . I spoke of societies with high social synergy where their institutions insure mutual advantage from their undertakings, and societies with low social synergy where the advantage of one individual becomes a victory over another, and the majority who are not victorious must shift as they can.[4]

Psychologist Abraham Maslow comments on Benedict:

> These societies have high synergy in which the social institutions are set up so as to transcend the polarity between selfishness and unselfishness, between self-interest and altruism, in which the person who is simply being selfish necessarily reaps rewards for himself. The society with high synergy is one in which virtue pays.[5]

The problem is, current society is in general not synergistic. Everything is divided into separate and, often, competing boxes. Our religions, our nation-states, our academic disciplines, our corporations are separate and do not see themselves as parts of a whole living system that is itself evolving toward the next stage of development.

To move toward a new and higher form of governance in the global village of the twenty-first century, we need to develop methods to enhance social synergy—methods that lead to ethical, "virtuous," choiceful evolution, in harmony with our environment, our social needs, and the evolutionary potential of our species.

At this stage, we do not need to depend exclusively on the transformation of human nature, although we expect it to happen, but also on developing a new social architecture for a "win-win," rather than a "zero-sum" game, in which when one group benefits, while the other loses and the rich get richer, and the poor get poorer. In her new book, *Building a Win-Win World: Life Beyond Global Economic Warfare*, Hazel Henderson examines how "our human potentials are finding expression in new forms of enterprise, institutions, partnerships, and cooperative agreements that can lead to the building of a win-win world."[6]

A high-synergy, or win-win, society becomes essential for human survival, given the increasing interdependence and creative/destructive powers of twenty-first century humanity. We have seen the horrible failures of twentieth-century efforts to force order on society. Nazism and Communism were grotesque distortions of the effort to create a higher order. They ignored the *law* that the ordering process reveals to us. That is, the new whole system must enhance freedom and consciousness, not suppress it. The new society we aim toward must increase our freedom and our consciousness, while freeing our unique creativity in such a way that it benefits the individual and the society.

I would like to describe a model to facilitate social synergy—a model that I have experimented with and find to be a demonstration of a more synergistic democracy. It is a preview of how order in the twenty-first century might operate.

The Synergistic Convergence Model (SYNCON)

It is the SYNCON model that is designed to foster our coming together as a whole. SYNCON stands for *syn*ergistic *con*vergence. It is a town meeting in the round. The Committee for the Future, which I co-founded, used to hold these three-day events in school auditoriums and ballrooms. We built a wheel-shaped environment divided into sections representing the basic functions of any community: environment; production; business; labor; agriculture; finance; governance; the social needs of health, education, and welfare; and technology. At the "growing edge" we had task forces in new capacities: the biological and healing revolution, the psychologies of growth, the information evolution, space development, new capacities in the physical sciences, and new theories in holistic political/economic systems.

The outer edge of the circle was represented by the arts. Artists, playwrights, poets, and dancers were asked to dramatize for the social body its struggle and its potential as a whole. A small task force at the very growing edge was called "Unexplained Phenomena." Here people who had unverifiable experiences, such as out-of-body, near-death, UFO, and so on, shared their insights. The SYNCON Wheel was designed to bring together a microcosm of humanity to function as a whole system, fulfilling the potential of all its members as parts of the whole community.

At the center of the Wheel was a space called "Coordination—Matching Needs and Resources." During the first SYNCON at Southern Illinois University, students built a spiral staircase at the center of the Wheel. I will never forget climbing the staircase, symbolic of a new cultural DNA, to witness below me the social body as a whole, in each of its separate functions, working to learn how to operate itself as one body.

During the process each task force, composed of experts and laypeople, stated its goals, needs, and resources. At the growing edge, the various task forces stated the actual potential in their fields—what could actually be accomplished if society were to encourage its genius to flourish as part of the whole. We had found that the genius at the growing edge felt as isolated as youngsters trapped in inner cities.

Then in a series of "mergers," various functional groups met to look for common goals and to match needs with resources. Synergy buzzed through the whole group. People linked rapidly with one another. Enthusiasm, excitement, and passion arose. It was palpable, especially among those who had been adversaries before. Hate can turn to love through synergy, as the field changes from repulsion to attraction and people get what they want through cocreation rather than codestruction. The dichotomy between selfishness and selflessness is transcended in self-actualization, as Maslow pointed out.

This dynamic search for common goals and the matching of people's needs with other people's resources was exciting, reaffirming, and empowering. It took attention off jockeying for power and adversarial techniques and win-lose tactics, where one "side" wins by putting the other down. In the Wheel, there were no "sides," just as there are not within our own bodies. The search for common goals, rather than for differences, reinforces holistic, win-win leadership and brings to the fore those who can see connections and find commonality. Often divisive leaders were set back by the gentle words of some non-power-oriented person who could see how a mutual benefit was possible. At the growing edge, the groups met to piece together the emerging potential of society as a whole. What would it be like if everything we knew could be predicted in the healing arts, in the psychologies of growth, in space and information evolution! The glory of our collective potential was being revealed among us as the social body struggled to coordinate itself as a whole, so that each part could "win" without being stopped or destroyed by another.

XII

224

XXI

TV cameras were used to record new agreements. Every night we played back the "New World's Evening News" and often were heard over local television with live call-ins. We transformed "news" from what is violent and breaking down to what is creative and breaking through. And we saw ourselves as the newsmakers, rather than as passive recipients and victims.

In the very end, we had an "All Walls Down" ceremony. People sang and danced. Often they formed a spontaneous spiral, as if the very ordering force of the universe were organizing and coordinating the social body as we took down the walls that divided us. Astronaut Edgar Mitchell was at one of the SYNCONS. He said, "If we had a spiritual Geiger counter, it would go off the charts!" Finally, after the music and movement lifted us, the group reassembled as a whole living body. The assembly was vibrating with life more abundant, for the whole is greater than the sum of its parts. The "greater than" is the additional energy required to provide what is needed without taking it away from anyone.

Each functional area restated its goals, needs, and resources. The adversarial mode of democracy, which is still win-lose, gave way to synergistic democracy, which is win-win. Robert's Rules of Parliamentary Order opened the way for very new and underdeveloped Synergistic Rules of Order. The social question to the whole assembly was, How could each member or group best realize its goals in such a way that others were also benefited or at least not hurt? If another was severely damaged, it meant *all* were hurt, for it was obvious in that moment we were all members of one body.

Finally, the questions were asked of the whole assembly: "Is anyone left out? Is anybody still hurting?" This is dangerous, for even one person can upset the harmony and coming together of the whole. We felt, however, that if someone was hurting, since that person was part of the body, it was the responsibility of the whole body to heal its own member. During the event, when people got upset with one another and wanted to reject someone from the Wheel, I asked: "Where are we going to reject them to? The prisons are filling up. We need to rebuild our communities and take people in wherever humanly possible. Only the very sick and the psycho- or sociopathic need to be kept apart, and that is a small minority."

I remember clearly at the first SYNCON, a young man who had been proposing the legalization of marijuana and who had been rejected by his task force, came into the center of the Wheel during the closing ceremony, kneeled down in his ragged jeans, and said, "It's going to be all right. This is what we meant all along."

Someone asked, "Where is religion in the Wheel?" The answer is, "Everywhere, and nowhere." The root of the word *religion* is *religare*, meaning "to bind back and make whole." When the social body comes together as a whole, it is Spirit that binds the parts, the same Spirit that synthesized the metals and minerals in our Earth, that organizes the cells in our bodies into stupendous communities of trillions of cells. This spiritual binding force is facilitated by a social structure which allows the natural to happen. The actual coming together is grace. Our part is to prepare the field. In that field, we all *do* come together by grace.

These SYNCONS brought to mind the awareness that the order for the twenty-first century will consist of synergistic social processes and structures which will allow each person and group to discover how to fulfill their own growth potential as parts of the whole, in freedom, guided by Spirit from within and connected through Spirit as the stimulus for mutual self-actualization and, ultimately, self-transcendence. When one becomes freely a part of the living whole, the separated self disappears and each of us partakes of the power and glory of the whole body.

I believe that the government of the future will not be world government. It will be genuine *self*-government. Higher Self-government. It will be a synergistic democracy, in which each person is free and responsible to be and do their best.

The next stage of self-governance will facilitate the individual to find his or her life purpose and to link our unique creativity to some need in the social body. We will experience the joy of cocreation, the passion of joining our genius and realizing our creative potential through self-rewarding action. Our motto, a modification of Thomas Jefferson's great statement, is this:

We hold this truth to be self-evident,
all people are born creative,
endowed by our Creator with the inalienable right and responsibility
to express our creativity
for the sake of ourselves and society as a whole.

227

Barbara Marx Hubbard is an author, futurist, social architect, public speaker, lecturer, and visionary. In 1984 her name was placed in nomination for the vice presidency of the United States with her campaign for a "Positive Future." She is a founding board member of the World Future Society and president of the Foundation for Conscious Evolution.

No less a visionary than R. Buckminster Fuller called her "the best-informed human now alive regarding futurism and the foresights it has produced."

In the 1970s, Barbara established the Committee for the Future in Washington, D.C., and since then has produced twenty-five major synergistic conferences to bring together opposing factions to seek cooperative solutions, a step toward a more cooperative democracy she calls "synocracy."

Barbara Marx Hubbard's books include the following: *Evolutionary Journey; The Hunger of Eve; The Revelation: A Message of Hope for the New Millennium;* and *Conscious Evolution.*

AFTERWORD

"Then the angel showed me the river of the water of life, bright as crystal, flowing from the throne of God and of the Lamb through the middle of the street of the city. On either side of the river is the tree of life with its twelve kinds of fruit, producing its fruit each month; and the leaves of the tree are for the healing of the nations."

—Revelation 22:1–2

A new heaven and a new earth are nigh. The pure life and substance of being flow through the center of our new life, nourishing all expressions of life, including the twelve divine ideas we have called "powers." Based in God and the Lamb of the Christ, this spiritual flow is grace in action and is healing all worldly divisions.

As the second millennium comes to a close and the third begins, this book has tried to show that true power is spiritual and originates within each of us. As we awaken to our Christ potential, we begin to realize the true greatness of our humanity. Emersed in the living waters flowing through the New Jerusalem, we see that the true destiny of humanity is not in technology, although there is nothing wrong with technology, but in the expression of our spiritual power.

229

The Apocalypse, fittingly, the other name for the book of Revelation, has also the meaning of "climactic doom," which of course is the image many millennialists are evoking. Yet Revelation is not about death but rebirth, the kindling of a whole new, higher life for humankind!

So how do we want to see it? Is the future half empty or half full? Is it the end times or a new beginning? The answer, for us, rests in our perception but also in our willingness "to change our minds," to repent. Thousands of years of being mere human beings isn't easy to release, even if destiny is calling for it. No habit is easy to break, but our authors have shown us the way: Not our will, but Thine be done.

Repent! The beginning is near!

FURTHER READING

If you would like to read further into the concept of the twelve powers, the following books are recommended. Some are totally devoted to the Fillmorean concept, others take their own approach, and several are devoted to inner powers within the body/mind without specifically being tied to the Unity model. Not all of these books are available from Unity School and some are out of print.

Anatomy of the Spirit: The Seven Stages of Power and Healing by Carolyn Myss, Ph.D., Harmony Books, New York, N.Y., 1996.

Christ Enthroned in Man by Cora Fillmore, Unity Books, Unity Village, Mo., 1988.

Christian Healing by Charles Fillmore, Unity Books, Unity Village, Mo., 1988.

The Healing Secrets of the Ages by Catherine Ponder, Parker Publishing Company, West Nyack, N.Y., 1967.

How to Use Your Twelve Gifts From God by William A. Warch, Christian Living Publishing Company, Anaheim, Calif., 1976.

Joy's Way: A Map for the Transformational Journey—An Introduction to the Potentials for Healing With Body Energies by W. Brugh Joy, M.D., J. P. Tarcher, Los Angeles, Calif., 1978.

Man and His Powers by Richard Lynch; Dodd, Mead, & Company, New York, N.Y., 1928.

Metaphysical Bible Dictionary, Unity Books, Unity Village, Mo., 1995.

Powers of the Soul by Ella Pomeroy, Island Press, New York, N.Y., 1948.

The Revealing Word by Charles Fillmore, Unity Books, Unity Village, Mo., 1997.

The Secret Teachings of All Ages by Manly P. Hall, The Philosophic Research Society, Los Angeles, Calif., 1952.

The Twelve Powers of Man by Charles Fillmore, Unity Books, Unity Village, Mo., 1995.

A Twelve-Power Meditation Exercise by Charles Roth, Unity Books, Unity Village, Mo., 1991.

Your God-Given Potential by Winifred Wilkinson Hausmann, Unity Books, Unity Village, Mo., 1978.

Your Power to Be by J. Sig Paulson, Doubleday & Company, Garden City, N.Y., 1969.

XII

232

XXI

NOTES

1. Charles Fillmore, *Keep a True Lent* (Unity Village: Unity Books, 1995), p. 46.

Introduction: Twelve Pathways to a New Millennium

1. William Irwin Thompson, *At the Edge of History* (New York: Harper & Row, 1971), p. 230.

2. Leonard Cohen, as quoted in George B. Leonard's *The Transformation: A Guide to the Inevitable Changes in Humankind* (New York: Delacorte Press, 1972), p. 1.

3. Doug Bottorff, *One World* (CD) (Unity Village: Unity School of Christianity, 1996).

4. Charles Fillmore, *The Twelve Powers of Man* (Unity Village: Unity Books, 1995), p. 15.

5. Alden Studebaker, *Wisdom for a Lifetime: How to Get the Bible Off the Shelf and Into Your Hands* (Unity Village: Unity Books, 1998).

Chapter 1, The Power of Love

1. Robert Browning, "Paracelsus," Part I, from *Masterpieces of Religious Verse* (New York: Harper & Brothers, 1948), p. 431.

Chapter 2, The Fire of Faith

1. Charles Fillmore, "Patience, the Fruit of Faith," *Weekly Unity*, January 16, 1972, p. 8, col. 1.

2. Whitall N. Perry (comp.), *A Treasury of Traditional Wisdom* (San Francisco: Harper & Row, 1986), p. 516.

3. Charles Fillmore, *Christian Healing* (Unity Village: Unity School of Christianity, 1988), p. 89.

4. Myrtle Fillmore, *Myrtle Fillmore's Healing Letters* (Unity Village: Unity School of Christianity, 1988), p. 70.

5. Thomas E. Witherspoon, *Myrtle Fillmore: Mother of Unity* (Unity Village: Unity Books, 1989), p. 274.

6. Peter Russell, *The Global Brain* (Los Angeles: Jeremy P. Tarcher, Inc., 1983), p. 71.

7. Ibid., p. 159.

8. Michael Murphy, *The Future of the Body* (Los Angeles: Jeremy P. Tarcher, Inc., 1992), p. 27–28.

9. Charles Fillmore, op. cit., p. 87.

Chapter 3, Understanding: Acceleration in Spiritual Information

1. Charles Fillmore, *The Revealing Word* (Unity Village: Unity Books, 1997), p. 201.

Chapter 10, Power Shift: A New Paradigm for the New Millennium

1. Barbara Marx Hubbard, *The Evolutionary Journey* (San Francisco: Evolutionary Press, 1982), p. 27.

2. Richard Tarnas, *The Passion of the Western Mind* (New York: Ballantine Books, 1991), pp. 214–215.

3. Ralph Lapp, *New York Times Magazine*, August 2, 1964, as quoted in *Bartlett's Familiar Quotations* (Boston: Little, Brown and Company, 1980), p. 764.

4. Gautama Buddha, *The Teachings of the Compassionate Buddha*, edited by E. A. Burtt (New York: The New American Library, 1955), p. 58.

5. Eknath Easwaran, *Gandhi the Man* (Tomales: Nilgiri Press, 1978), p. 152.

6. Lao Tsu, *Tao Te Ching*, Translation by Gia-fu Feng and Jane English (New York: Vintage Books, 1989), verse 73.

7. H. Emilie Cady, *Lessons in Truth* (Unity Village: Unity Books, 1995), p. 78.

CHAPTER 12, DISCOVERY OF A NEW ORDERING OF THE FUTURE

1. Peter Russell, *The White Hole in Time* (San Francisco: HarperSan-Francisco, 1992), p. 211.

2. James Redfield, *The Tenth Insight: Holding the Vision* (New York: Warner Books, 1996), p. 217.

3. Ralph H. Abraham, *Chaos, Gaia, Eros* (San Francisco: HarperSan-Francisco, 1996), p. 68.

4. Ruth Benedict, "SYNERGY: Patterns of Good Culture," *American Anthropologist*, 1970, 72:320–33. Also see T. George Harris, "About Ruth Benedict and Her Lost Manuscript," *Psychology Today*, 1970, 4:51–52.

5. Abraham H. Maslow, *The Farther Reaches of Human Nature* (New York: The Viking Press, 1971), p. 194.

6. Hazel Henderson, *Building a Win-Win World: Life Beyond Global Economic Warfare* (San Francisco: Berrett-Koehler Publishers, 1996), p. 3.

Printed in U.S.A.

1-2894-15M-1-98